Dear Mary.

This book that I give to you is an awkward and unwieldy volume to handle, but I assure you that the series of stories it contains are intensely interesting and the pictures with which the stories are illustrated are apt indicators of the life of the different classes of people of whom the stories are told. In the perusal of the stories you will get great pleasure and gain much valuable information as they narrate quite correctly the history of the settlement of the North American Colonies and the first years of our national life.

Hoping that you may get from the book the pleasure and knowledge I anticipate,

I am your hopeful

Grandpa

Christmas, 1923.

Howard Pyle's Book of
The American Spirit

Books By
HOWARD PYLE

Howard Pyle's Book of the American Spirit
Howard Pyle's Book of Pirates
Men of Iron
A Modern Aladdin
Pepper and Salt
The Ruby of Kishmoor
Stolen Treasure
The Wonder Clock

Harper & Brothers, *Publishers*
Established 1817

La Salle Christening the Country "Louisiana"

Illustration from
THE GREAT LA SALLE
by Henry Loomis Nelson
Originally published in
HARPER'S MAGAZINE, *February*, 1905

Howard Pyle's Book of The American Spirit

The Romance of American History
Pictured by Howard Pyle ✑
Compiled by Merle Johnson: with
Narrative Descriptive Text from
Original Sources *Edited by*
Francis J. Dowd

Harper & Brothers *Publishers*
New York & London MCMXXIII

HOWARD PYLE'S BOOK OF
THE AMERICAN SPIRIT

CONTENTS

PART I

COMING OF THE ENGLISH AND THE DUTCH

PART II

THE FRENCH COME UPON THE SCENE

PART III

THE NATION

ILLUSTRATIONS

Illustrations

Illustrations

[ix]

Illustrations

Illustrations

Illustrations

Illustrations

FOREWORD

THE title of this volume was not chosen idly—it was chosen because these Howard Pyle pictures *do* breathe an *American Spirit*. Beyond the technical excellence which has caused artists to treasure proofs of these pictures, beyond the unquestioned accuracy of costume and setting, is the spiritual, personal something that makes pictures live. Pyle furnishes a window into our American past as given by no word historian: wholesome, homely, full of interest.

The instant success of Howard Pyle's *Book of Pirates*, a bringing together of previously scattered material, gives certainty that this similar compilation will be of value. With Francis J. Dowd, who furnishes the text, I am proud to assist in presenting in such fine form the work of a Great American, Howard Pyle.

MERLE JOHNSON.

Part I
Coming of the English and the Dutch

Chapter I

VIRGINIA—THE FIRST PERMANENT ENGLISH SETTLEMENT IN AMERICA

"UP to the last third of the sixteenth century," to quote from Tyler's *England in America*, "American history was the history of Spanish conquest, settlement, and exploration. Except for the feeble Portuguese settlements in Brazil and at the mouth of the La Plata, from Florida and the Gulf of Mexico, around the eastern and western coasts of South America, and northward to the Gulf of California, all was Spanish—mainland and islands alike." With the opening of the next century England and France were destined to compete for the New World.

"While English colonization at first sprang out of rivalry with Spain" and afterwards with France, "and was late in beginning, England's claims in America were hardly later than Spain's," for only five years after the voyage of Columbus, in 1492, "John Cabot, under an English charter, reached the continent of North America," seeking, as Columbus had, a new route to the far East—the predominating motive of all the early explorers.

"About 1530," Tyler continues, "William Hawkins visited the coast of Guinea, and in 1562 Sir John Hawkins, following in the track of his father," visited the same region, and, obtaining there a cargo of negroes, brought them to Hispaniola. Selling the slaves

[1]

to the planters there, he returned to England with a rich cargo of the products of Hispaniola. "In 1564 Hawkins repeated the experiment with greater success, and on his way home he relieved the struggling

From *Harper's
Magazine*
February, 1890

THE GOVERNOR GREETS MORGAN

This event occurred upon the arrival in Jamaica of Henry Morgan, chief of England's Buccaneer captains, a man after Drake's own heart, who raided the Spanish possessions between 1668 and 1671.

French colony of Laudonnière," which Admiral Coligny had planted in Florida the year before, and which the Spaniards barbarously destroyed soon after Hawkins's departure.

SIR FRANCIS DRAKE

In the expedition which Hawkins made in 1567 to the West Indies one of the two ships which escaped when

[2]

the fleet was attacked by the Spaniards in the harbor of San Juan de Ulloa was commanded by a young man named Francis Drake, who was destined to become the greatest seaman of his age. "From the time of that disaster Drake," as Higginson writes in *The Old English Seamen*, "took up almost as a profession the work of plundering the Spaniards; and he might well be called a buccaneer had he not concentrated his piracy on one particular nation. He was the son of a Protestant chaplain who had suffered for his opinions; and though the policy of Elizabeth was long uncertain, the public sentiment of England was with the United Netherlands in their desperate war against Philip II. The English seamen had found out that the way to reach Spain was through her rich possessions in West India and South America, or by plundering the treasure ships to which she could afford but meager escort. Drake made one trip after another to the American coast, and on February 11, 1573, he looked for the first time on the Pacific, from the top of a tree in Panama. He resolved to become the pioneer of England on the ocean where the English flag had never floated, and he asked the blessing of God on this enterprise. In November, 1577, he embarked for the fulfilment of this purpose, being resolved to take Peru itself from the Spaniards. His enterprise was known at the time as 'the famous voyage,' and ended in the first English circumnavigation of the globe.

"Such novels as Kingsley's *Westward Ho!* or *Sir Amyas Leigh* give a picture, hardly exaggerated, of the exciting achievements of these early seamen. Drake sailed from Plymouth, November 15, 1577, with one hundred and sixty-four sailors and adventurers in a fleet of five ships and barks, and after making some captures of Spanish vessels about the Cape de Verd Islands he steered for the open sea. He was fifty-four days out of sight of land—time enough to have made six ocean voyages in a Liverpool steamer—before he came in sight of the Brazils. There he cruised awhile and victualed his ships with seals, which are not now considered good eating. Following down the coast in the track of Magellan, he reached at last the strait which bears the name of this Portuguese explorer,

[3]

but which no Englishman had yet traversed. Drake's object was to come by this unexpected ocean route to Peru, and there ravage the Spanish settlements.

"Reaching the coast of Chile, he heard from an Indian in a canoe that there was a great Spanish ship at Santiago laden with

From *Harper's Magazine*, January, 1883

"THOMAS MOON BEGAN TO LAY ABOUT HIM WITH HIS SWORD"

treasure from Peru. Approaching the port, the Englishmen found the ship riding at anchor, having on board but six Spaniards and three negroes. These poor fellows, never dreaming that any but their own countrymen could have found their way there, welcomed the visitors, beating a drum in their honor and setting forth a jar of

[4]

Chilean wine for their entertainment. But as soon as the strangers entered, one of them, named Thomas Moon, began to lay about him with his sword in a most uncivil manner, striking one Spaniard, and shouting, '*Abaxo, perro!*' ('Go down, dog!'). All the Spaniards and negroes were at once driven below, except one, who jumped overboard and alarmed the town. The people of Santiago fled to the woods, and the Englishmen landed and robbed the town, including a little chapel, from which they took 'a silver challice, two cruets, and one altar-cloth, the spoyle whereof our Generall gave to M. Fletcher, his minister.' On board the captured ship they found abundance of wine and treasure, amounting to 37,000 ducats of Spanish money—a ducat being worth five and a half shillings English."

Drake did not think it prudent to go home by the way he had come, and, Higginson continues, "resolved to avoid the Strait of Magellan, which he had found dangerous, and the Atlantic Ocean, where he was too well known, and to go northward along the coast, and sail across the Pacific, as he had already crossed the Atlantic. He sailed as far north as California, which he called New Albion; he entered 'a faire and good bay,' which may have been that of San Francisco; he took possession of the country in the name of Queen Elizabeth, setting up a post with that announcement. Then he sailed across the Pacific, this passage lasting from midsummer until October 18 [1579], when he and his men came among the islands off the coast of Africa, and so rounded the Cape of Good Hope, and reached England [in November, 1580], after three years' absence. They were the first Englishmen to sail round the world and the first of their countrymen to visit those islands of 'the gorgeous East' which Portugal had first reached, and Spain had now wrested from Portugal."

The Queen received him with undisguised favor, and met a request from Philip II for Drake's surrender by knighting the freebooter and wearing in her crown the jewel he offered her as a present. "The revenge," says Tyler, "that Drake had taken for the affair at San Juan de Ulloa was so complete that for more than a hundred years he was spoken of in Spanish annals as 'the Dragon.'"

[5]

DRAKE'S ATTACK UPON SAN DOMINGO

When once again the tumults of war arose, "Sir Francis Drake," says Higginson, "was summoned to lead a great naval expedition, a real 'armada,' to the attack on Spanish America. He sailed from Plymouth, England, September 17, 1585, with twenty-five vessels, carrying twenty-three hundred men, and he had under him, as vice-admiral, Capt. Martin Frobisher, famous by his endeavor after the northwest passage. I must pass lightly over the details of Drake's enterprise. It was full of daring, though it must be remembered that the Spanish forts in the West Indies were weak, their ordnance poor, and their garrisons small. At the city of San Domingo, which is described as 'the antientest and chief inhabited place in all the tract of country hereabout,' Drake landed a thousand or twelve hundred men. A hundred cavalrymen hovered near them, but quickly retreated; the thousand Englishmen divided in two portions, assaulted the two city gates, carried them easily, and then reunited in the market place. Toward midnight they tried the gates of the castle; it was at once abandoned, and by degrees, street by street, the invaders got possession of half the town. The Spanish commissioners held the other half, and there were constant negotiations for ransom; 'but upon disagreement,' says the English narrator, 'we still spent the early mornings in firing the outmost houses; but they being built very magnificently of stone, with high lofts, gave us no small travail to ruin them.' They kept two hundred sailors busy at this work of firing houses, while as many soldiers stood guard over them; and yet had not destroyed more than a third part of the town when they consented to accept twenty-five thousand ducats for the ransom of the rest."

Besides Drake there were many other daring English mariners, and among these adventurous men were Sir Humphrey Gilbert and his half brother, Sir Walter Raleigh. Gilbert obtained a patent in 1578 to plant a colony in America, but bad fortune attended him, and on his third voyage, in 1583, he himself, with his ship and all on board, was lost on the way home.

[6]

Gilbert's work was then taken up by Raleigh, who, although he never himself set foot in America, fitted out three different

From *Harper's Magazine*, January, 1883
DRAKE'S ATTACK UPON SAN DOMINGO

expeditions for those shores in the years 1584–87. The two ships that he sent out in 1584 reached the coast of North Carolina. So

[7]

glowing a report did the voyagers make of the new lands upon their return that Queen Elizabeth had them named "Virginia," in her honor. The next expedition sent out by Raleigh in 1585 consisted of seven ships with nearly two hundred settlers on board. They landed on the island of Roanoke, but the colony did not prosper, and in the summer of 1586 Sir Francis Drake, returning from the Spanish Main, succored the imperilled colonists and carried them home in his ships. A day or two after their departure, a ship sent by Raleigh arrived, and about two weeks later three ships under Sir Richard Grenville, Raleigh's admiral, came. After hunting in vain for the first settlers, Grenville returned to England, fifteen men remaining behind to retain possession. In less than another year Raleigh sent out a third fleet for Roanoke with one hundred and fifty settlers, among them the painter, John White, whom he made governor. Two months after their arrival the governor's daughter, wife of Ananias Dare, gave birth to a daughter, Virginia, who was the first child to be born in America of English parents.

Ten days after the birth of his granddaughter, Governor White was forced to go to England for supplies. He was unable to put to sea again until March, 1591, having been delayed by his taking part in the great battle fought in the English Channel in which the Spanish Armada was completely destroyed. Reaching Roanoke Island finally in August of that year, he made diligent search for the settlers, but could find no trace of them, and their disappearance is shrouded in mystery even to this day.

Meanwhile, James I succeeding Elizabeth, Raleigh lost the royal favor and, having been convicted of high treason, he was deprived of the charter which had given him a monopoly of American colonization.

After Raleigh's downfall the Virginia Company, under whose auspices the first permanent English colony was made in America, was formed. In this first Virginia charter, obtained from King James in 1606, provision was made, says Tyler, "for the incorporation of two companies, one consisting of 'certain knights, gentlemen, mer-

[8]

chants' in and about London, and the other of 'sundry knights, gentlemen, merchants' in and about Plymouth."

The first expedition sent out by the company in August, 1606, having been unsuccessful, a second fleet sailed from Plymouth, May 31, 1607, with one hundred and twenty settlers. They landed at the mouth of the Kennebec River, in Maine, August 18, 1607. These colonists were soon discouraged and all but forty-five men went back to England in the ships when they returned in December. Of the forty-five men who did remain, so terrible was the winter of 1607–08 that they, too, returned in the spring.

"To the London Company, therefore, though slower in starting" (Tyler, *England in America*), "belongs the honor of the first permanent English colony in America." The ships sailed from London, December 20, 1606, and on April 26, 1607, the colonists sighted the capes of Virginia, which they named Henry and Charles, for the sons of the king. For more than two weeks they sought a place of settlement, and after naming the broad river which opened beyond Hampton Roads the James, at length they landed, May 14, 1607, about thirty-two miles from its mouth; and to the village which was built there they gave the name of Jamestown.

At first the colonists were in high spirits, but disaster was not far away. Their supplies were low, the site selected unhealthful, and, more than half of the little company being "gentlemen," there were very few to do the manual labor necessary. Starvation and disease threatened them constantly, and within six months one-third of their number were dead. But for Capt. John Smith, the ablest man among them, who in his *True Relation* has left us an account of their trials and adventures, the entire little band would have perished.

During the next twelve years, though the "starving time" more than once threatened, under the leadership of able men like Sir Thomas Dale and Sir George Yeardley, the colony soon got on its feet; and with the introduction of tobacco culture and the institution of private property industry was stimulated and a period of prosperity set in.

LANDING OF NEGROES AT JAMESTOWN FROM A DUTCH MAN-OF-WAR, 1619

"In those days slave dealing," says Thomas A. Janvier in "The Evolution of New York" (*Harper's Magazine*, May, 1893), "was an important and well-thought-of industry—or, in the more elegant phrase of one of the gravest of New York historians, 'a species of maritime adventure then engaged in by several of our most respectable merchants.' The Dutch are credited with having brought the first cargo of slaves to the northern part of America—from their possessions on the Guinea coast to the Virginia plantations—and a regular part of the business of the Dutch West India Company was providing African slaves for use in its American colonies. The profits of the business—even allowing for the bad luck of a high death rate on the western passage—was so alluringly great that it was not one to be slighted by the eminently go-ahead merchants of New Amsterdam."

"In 1619, the year Sir George Yeardley came to set up an assembly, and thus establish government by the people for the first time," writes Woodrow Wilson in his *History of the American People*, "another very notable thing also happened. A Dutch man-of-war came into the river and sold twenty negroes to the colonists as slaves. A handful of slaves made no great difference at first; they were so few as scarcely to affect the life of the colony, and it was to be many a long day before their number was much added to. But their coming was the beginning of a great change which was slowly, very slowly, to alter the whole face of society in the settlements."

"In 1621" (Higginson, *History of the United States*), "came a more desirable accession, through the shipment, by the Virginia Company of London, of 'respectable young women' for wives of those colonists who would pay the cost of transportation—at first one hundred and twenty pounds of tobacco, afterward one hundred and fifty. In July, 1620, the colony was four thousand strong and shipped to England forty thousand pounds of tobacco. This was

Landing of Negroes at Jamestown from a Dutch
Man-of-war, 1619

Illustration from
COLONIES AND NATION
by Woodrow Wilson

Originally published in
HARPER'S MAGAZINE, *January,* 1901

raised with the aid of many bound apprentices—boys and girls picked up in the streets of London and sent out—and of many 'disorderly persons' sent by order of the king."

In the last years of his reign King James, not liking the Puritan element in control of the Virginia Company, and liking even less their granting, a few years before, an extension of representative

From *Harper's Magazine*, April, 1883
ARRIVAL OF THE YOUNG WOMEN AT JAMESTOWN, 1621

government, annulled the company's charter and in 1624 made Virginia a royal colony.

Among the royal governors, the most faithful to king and church was Sir William Berkeley, who had the longest rule of any man in Colonial history. Beginning in 1642, he governed Virginia for the king until 1677, except during the years (1652–60) of the Commonwealth. Charles I was England's king during the first seven years

[12]

of Sir William's rule, and when he was executed in 1649, Berkeley and his followers remained faithful to the crown and sought to hold Virginia for the second Charles, then an exile in Europe. But, as we shall see in Chapter III, he was forced to yield the government to Cromwell's commissioners.

Chapter II

FOUNDING OF PLYMOUTH AND MASSACHUSETTS

HE English were now firmly established in Virginia, but thus far all efforts to build a colony in New England had failed. Capt. John Smith had visited the New England coast in 1614, with some private adventurers, with a view to colonization, but the result was once more only the old story of misfortune, which caused him to write "that he was not so foolish as to suppose that anything but the prospect of great gain would induce people to settle in such a place."

A people, however, whom we are now to consider, were to come to New England's inhospitable shores—with the prospect of great gain, to be sure, but of a quite different kind than that which Smith had in mind. This little band of daring, religious spirits— the Pilgrim Fathers, as they have always been called—separating for conscience' sake from the Church of England, had left England for Holland, and dwelt in that place of refuge for twelve years. Yet, in spite of the kindness of their Dutch neighbors, Holland was not England by long odds. They saw their children growing up and taking on the habits and speech of their neighbors, becoming more Dutch every day. Besides, the truce between Holland and Spain was nearing its end and a new war threatened. These reasons, together with their desire to do something "for the propagating and advancing of the Gospel of Christ in remote parts of the world," finally made them resolve, Woodrow Wilson writes in his *History of the American People*, "to try their fortune in the New World, where Virginia had now become fairly established and seemed secure of

[14]

its future." Their purpose thus determined, they selected a hundred of their younger and stronger men and women to go to America.

THE LANDING OF THE PILGRIMS, 1620

The Pilgrim party left Delft Haven for England in July, 1620, and one hundred and two of those who came from Leyden sailed in the *Mayflower* on September 6th following. The vessel first anchored in Cape Cod, in what is now the harbor of Provincetown, where nearly all the party went ashore. A permanent landing place was selected, where New Plymouth was built. Most of the women and children remained on the vessel until log huts were built for their reception, and it was March 21, 1621, before the survivors were all landed.

"It was the month of September, 1620" (Wilson, *History of the American People*), "before those who could go, a hundred and two in all, got fairly upon their way, in a single small vessel, the *Mayflower*. Mr. Brewster went with them, as their leader, but Mr. Robinson stayed behind; for the greater number remained to await a later opportunity, and wished to keep their pastor with them.

"Stress of weather kept the little *Mayflower* nine weeks on the Atlantic; and when at last, in the bleak days of late November, they sighted land, it turned out to be Cape Cod, not the Virginia coast at all. The master of the ship had let his reckonings go wrong, was many leagues north of the landfall he had been instructed to make, by way of the Bay of Delaware, and found himself, as he closed with the coast he had blindly come upon, involved in shoals from which he did not very well know how safely to extricate himself. The Virginia Company had been divided into two bodies, as Mr. Brewster's people knew very well, and the gentlemen in London from whom they had got their charter had no rights over this northern coast. It belonged now to the separate 'Plymouth branch' of the Company. The immigrants had half a mind to make for Hudson's River, after all. But the season was late and stormy, and the captain surly and unwilling, and they determined to land where they were and make the best of what they had hit upon. They took care

first, however, to make some sort of government ready for the
landing; their charter from the Virginia Company being no longer

From *Harper's Magazine*, December, 1883
"THE MASTER CAUSED VS TO HAVE SOME BEERE"

By the irony of fate the Puritans reached the New World at Christmas time. But to them Christmas was a survival of the old pagan Saturnalia, and on Christmas day they went on shore to build their
first house for common use, while on that day all other Christians in the world stayed their hands
from toil. "Monday the 25th being Christmas-day," says Mourt, "we began to drinke water aboord,
but at night the master caused vs to have some Beere."

The Landing of the Pilgrims

Illustration from
AN ENGLISH NATION
by Thomas Wentworth Higginson

Originally published in
HARPER'S MAGAZINE, *April*, 1883

[17]

serviceable, and a few even of their little group of settlers being persons taken aboard in England who were not of their congregation—and not certain, therefore, to submit without compulsion to be governed by their authority and discipline—they judged it best to draw up an agreement before going ashore, by which all should bind themselves to accept the authority of their leaders until, at any rate, they should obtain a grant of lands and of power from the Plymouth Company, upon whose coasts they were thus unexpectedly to be set down. That done, they were ready to make their landing and see what sort of a home the new coast would afford them.

"Several weeks elapsed before a suitable place was found for landing and erecting shelter, and even then it was only 'the best they could find'—the quiet harbor, within a little bay, upon which Captain Smith had written 'Plymouth' on the map he had sketched as he passed that way, putting into bays and examining harbors with businesslike curiosity six years before. January had come, and the first rigors of winter, before they got to work to put up shelter. Happily, the winter was mild, though icy cold, for all that. The strenuous work and cruel exposure of those first weeks, which wearily lengthened into months ere spring came, and the poor and insufficient food eked out from their scant supplies, brought upon them agues, fevers, scurvy, and all the other distempers that want and exposure bring, and they saw what the settlers at Jamestown had seen of the pitiless power of the wilderness. Before that dreadful season of suffering had passed full half of their number were dead, Mr. Carver among the rest, and they had seen a time when there were but six or seven sound persons among them all to care for the scores who were stricken. But they were steadfast, as always. They elected Mr. Bradford governor in the stead of Mr. Carver, and went on as they could with their fight to live. They knew of no place to which to go back, and no one asked to go with the *Mayflower* when she set sail for England again in April."

"These" (Thomas Hutchinson, *History of Massachusetts*), "were the founders of the Colony of Plymouth. The settlement of this

[18]

Mary Dyer Brought Before Governor Endicott

In 1635 Mary Dyer was one of the prominent supporters of Anne Hutchinson in the Antinomian controversy, and, with others of the cult, was driven from Massachusetts. She and her husband went to Rhode Island. Later returning to England, she remained there three years, and during her stay became a convert to Quakerism. In 1658 she began to preach the Quaker doctrines in the Colony of New Haven and was banished. Then she went to Boston, and in September, 1659, she was arrested and imprisoned with other Quakers. She was banished, on pain of death should she return.

Illustration from
THE HANGING OF MARY DYER
by Basil King
Originally published in
McClure's Magazine, *November,* 1906

colony occasioned the settlement of Massachusetts Bay, which was the source of all the other colonies of New England. Virginia was in a dying state, and seemed to revive and flourish from the example of New England. I am not preserving from oblivion the names of heroes whose chief merit is the overthrow of cities, provinces, and empires, but the names of the founders of a flourishing town and colony, if not of the whole British empire in America."

The years immediately following the settlement made at Plymouth by the *Mayflower* pioneers saw other scattered settlements spring up along the shores of Massachusetts Bay. Among these was the unsuccessful attempt made by Thomas Weston to establish a colony at Wessagusett, the modern Weymouth, in 1622. He was followed in the same year by Thomas Morton, who, with thirty others, sought to found an Episcopal colony as agent for Sir Ferdinando Gorges. But the most important of all these attempts, and the one which led directly to the founding of Massachusetts by the Puritans, was that of the little fishing settlement made at Cape Ann in 1623 by the Dorchester adventurers. After their arrival, however, trouble arose with men from Plymouth already there, among whom was Roger Conant, an independent settler. Abandoning the Cape Ann site, they went with Conant to Naumkeag and there set up a settlement which became the later city of Salem. Soon strong support came to them from England, due to the interest of the Rev. John White, a merchant as well as a preacher. He secured for them a patent from the Council for New England, under which there came into being a powerful association, whose aid was to give the enterprise greater promise than had ever been anticipated.

JOHN ENDICOTT CUTS THE CROSS OUT OF THE ENGLISH FLAG, 1634

As a result the company organized at London, June 20, 1628, for the purpose of attempting a settlement in America sent out a party of emigrants under John Endicott, who arrived September 6th at Naumkeag, afterward called Salem. Endicott, "a blunt, passionate, wilful man," was hard to deal with, but as he was the most efficient man the company could find, he was chosen governor. Upon landing, he found only a few settlers, Roger Conant and others, part of them strays from Plymouth, who were quite disposed to be impatient of his authority. His government early laid down the lines of policy which Massachusetts was to follow for many years afterward. From the very beginning it was evident that he would have no dealings with the ungodly in the colony; and, accordingly, within three months after his arrival he crossed the bay to the settlement which Captain Wollaston had established in 1625, and proceeded to hew down the Maypole which had been erected there by Thomas Morton, who had changed the name of the settlement of Wollaston to "Merry Mount" and "planted a Maypole eighty feet high, around which, for many days together, the setlers 'frisked' hand in hand with the Indian girls."

In 1629 the company in England obtained a charter and became known as "The Governor and Company of Massachusetts Bay in New England." John Winthrop was appointed governor to supersede Endicott, and arrived at Salem, June 12, 1630, after a long, stormy voyage.

Winthrop, finding Endicott's colony in "a sad and unexpected condition" and not being favorably impressed with the country around Salem, established himself with most of the newcomers at Charlestown, which had been laid out and named by Endicott. Winthrop followed the policy laid down by Endicott at Salem, making, as Endicott had done, a confession of the faith and drawing up a church covenant with Dudley and Isaac Johnson, one of the assistants. Then they associated themselves with others and so established the Congregational Church, making God's word the law of the state, the interpretation of which became the function of the clergy.

Winthrop and his assistants at once took measures to show their authority, and when Morton of "Merry Mount," whom Endicott had once banished, showed defiance to their authority, he was arrested and sent prisoner to England, his goods being seized and his house burned. In spite, however, of the troubles that beset the

Endicott Cutting the Cross Out of the English Flag

Illustration from
AN ENGLISH NATION
by Thomas Wentworth Higginson

Originally published in
HARPER'S MAGAZINE, *April,* 1883

colony under Winthrop, "before the winter of 1631, the towns scattered through Massachusetts were eight in number—Salem, Charlestown, Dorchester, Boston, Watertown, Roxbury, Mystic, and Lynn" (Tyler, *England in America*).

The basis of citizenship became church membership and the Bible was the only law book recognized by Winthrop and his assistants. Persons "that were unmeet to inhabit here" and consequently "deemed inimical to the accepted state of affairs were punished with banishment from the colony."

The evident purpose of the Massachusetts colony to throw off their allegiance to the mother country at the first favorable opportunity became more and more apparent, and when, in 1634, owing to more rigorous enforcement in England of the laws against Nonconformists by Laud, Archbishop of Canterbury, the immigration to New England assumed immense volume, including so many of the best, "both ministers and Christians," the king and Archbishop Laud became aroused to the danger threatened by Massachusetts. A demand was made by the Privy Council to hand in the Massachusetts charter, and a new commission—the Commission for Foreign Plantations—with the Archbishop of Canterbury at its head, was appointed for the government of the colonies.

At this momentous crisis in the history of the colony, Dudley, the then governor, replied that the charter could be returned only by command of the General Court, which was not then in session. "In this moment of excitement the figure of Endicott again dramatically crosses the stage of history. Conceiving an intense dislike to the cross in the English flag, he denounced it as antichrist, and cut it out with his own hands from the ensign borne by the Company at Salem. Endicott was censured by the General Court for the act, but soon the cross was left out of all flags except that of the fort at Castle Island, in Boston Harbor" (*England in America*). The flag had been given by the pope to a former king of England as an ensign of victory, and Endicott had so worked upon the minds of many citizens that they would not follow the standard with the cross upon it.

The Puritan Governor Interrupting the
Christmas Sports

Illustration from
CHRISTMAS
by George William Curtis

Originally published in
HARPER'S MAGAZINE, *December,* 1883

The Massachusetts General Court continued to disregard the demands made on them to surrender the charter, until in 1642, the war between king and Parliament breaking out, Endicott and his companions in Massachusetts were left free to work out their own destinies.

Far more dangerous, however, than the demand to annul the Massachusetts charter were the dissensions which now arose among the colonists themselves, owing to the lack of real unity in church matters. The majority of the inhabitants had had little or no say in the form of religion that had been adopted in the colony, and soon a spirit of resistance was aroused against the stringent limitations which were placed on thought and religious practice. None but members of the Congregational Church could vote or hold office; thus "God's" word was the law of the state, the Church and state were one, and the magistrates were the pillars of the church.

Among those who ran counter to this aristocracy of saints—this religious despotism—was Roger Williams, who, among other things, denied the right of the magistrates to dictate what men should believe and what form of worship they should follow. He also preached against the union of Church and state; and finally, when he refused to take the oath of fidelity to the provincial charter, he so excited the wrath of the government that he was ordered to leave the colony.

ANNE HUTCHINSON PREACHES IN HER HOUSE IN BOSTON, 1637

Scarcely had Roger Williams left the scene when another came to cause new and even greater perplexities to the Massachusetts magistrates. Henry Cabot Lodge says in his *Short History of the English Colonies in America* the fresh troubles that now broke out at Boston "arose from the actions and sayings of Mrs. Hutchinson, an active, energetic, uneasy woman, who had followed Cotton to America some years before. Her brother-in-law, Wheelwright, soon settled at Mount Wollaston, was her chief ally, and Mrs. Hutchinson herself propounded various doctrines which were at variance with those generally accepted. She held lectures for women, and assailed

Anne Hutchinson Preaching in Her
House in Boston

Illustration from
COLONIES AND NATION
by Woodrow Wilson

Originally published in
HARPER'S MAGAZINE, *February*, 1901

[25]

the ministers—especially Wilson of the Boston church—accusing them of being under a covenant of works, not of grace, and satirizing their sermons. Loud and bitter controversies sprang up. Mrs. Hutchinson obtained the powerful support of Vane [recently elected governor] and of Dummer and Coddington, and, to a certain extent, of Cotton. Boston was in a ferment of excitement. Wilson, the pastor of the Boston church, where the Hutchinsonians were in the majority, was attacked and censured; and at the next meeting of the court the ministers also assembled and a fast was ordered. The ministers decided in conclave that for heresy and error the court might proceed without tarrying for the Church; and thereupon Wheelwright, for a sermon preached during the fast, was adjudged guilty of sedition by the court, although the governor, some members of the House, and the people of Boston protested. The next court for general elections was held in the open air at Newtown, where Winthrop and Dudley were chosen governor and deputy, and the Hutchinsonians were left off the board of assistants. After a scene of great violence, the old party, backed by the ministers and the country members, prevailed. Vane behaved petulantly and angrily, and, after some further controversy with Winthrop, left the country forever. The sentence of Wheelwright was deferred; a synod of ministers was held, eighty-two points of doctrine held by members of the Hutchinsonian party were condemned, and it looked as if peace would return without resort to stronger measures. But in the autumn the controversy broke out once more; Wheelwright's sermon was again called in question, and, as its author was contumacious, he was disfranchised and banished and soon after betook himself to the Piscataqua. Mrs. Hutchinson was then sent for and, after a stormy trial and fierce altercations, was likewise sentenced to banishment, and during the winter confined in her house, where she was visited by the clergy and gradually retracted her doctrines, but asserted that much had been falsely attributed to her. This led to fresh controversy; the government finally interfered, a warrant was issued for her expulsion from the jurisdiction, and she departed to Rhode Island. Some of her sympathizers

Mary Dyer Refuses to Repent of Her Quaker Principles

Banished in September, 1654, she again returned to Massachusetts in October of the same year, whereupon she was at once sentenced to death. The authorities, however, relenting, she was reprieved and again banished, but only after being compelled to witness the hanging of two other Quakers. In May of the following year she again appeared in Boston and was once more condemned to death by Governor Endicott, and hanged on Boston Common, June 1, 1660.

Illustration from
THE HANGING OF MARY DYER
by Basil King

Originally published in
McClure's Magazine, *November, 1906*

followed her, some were disarmed and banished, but most of them recanted and made submission. The case of Roger Williams was political; that of Mrs. Hutchinson was both political and religious. Her peculiar doctrines and her sharp criticisms aroused the undying hostility of the clergy, the most powerful class in the community; while the action of Vane and his friends associated her with the opposition to the old leaders. An attack upon the Church, in a community where Church and state were identical, was an attack upon the state; and the fierce dissension which she caused was a source of danger to a colony in perpetual peril from English foes. The government drove her from their jurisdiction—as they had a perfect right to do—because the clergy hated her and because they believed the safety of the state required it. There is no doubt that it was a vigorous and arbitrary suppression of freedom of speech and opinion, and the only question is whether, politically and as a matter of expediency, the government's high-handed measures were justified by circumstances. No one who looks at the matter from the point of view of the year 1637, and not from that of the nineteenth century, can hesitate in answering the question in the affirmative. The strong policy of repression, at all events, answered its purpose, and peace, quiet, and safety were restored. The colony prospered, legislation was improved, and courts extended; while three thousand additional settlers arrived."

THE QUAKERS AND THE PURITANS

Many new religious sects arose during the Puritan epoch, and most famous among them was the Society of Friends, or Quakers. The name "Quakers" was given them in 1650, when their founder, George Fox, having been brought before a justice at Derby, England, for disturbing the peace by his preaching, told the magistrate to "quake before the Lord." Persecuted in England, the Quakers sought refuge in America, where for a time every effort was made, especially in Massachusetts, to crush them. These men held extreme democratic principles. They taught that all men were equal, that reverence was due only to God, not to man; and they refused to swear allegiance to governments, because the Bible commanded to "swear not at all."

A QUAKER EXHORTER IN NEW ENGLAND

Having driven out Roger Williams and Mrs. Hutchinson, the Massachusetts authorities, who demanded that all persons should show the highest respect to those in power, were not likely to admit these people. It was about twenty years after the Hutchinson episode that the first Quakers appeared in Massachusetts, in the person of Mary Fisher and Ann Austin, who arrived at Boston in 1656. They were promptly cast into prison, their persons stripped to see if any body marks of witches might be found, and then they were shipped back to Barbadoes on the same vessel that brought them. Others who followed them, some coming from Rhode Island, where they were tolerated, suffered a like fate. They reviled, scolded, and denounced the authorities in Church and state, calling the magistrates "hirelings" and "seed of the serpent." As a result severe laws were passed providing for their banishment, with a penalty of death if they returned. Some did return "to seek martyrdom" in New England; they came to Massachusetts especially to "test the law," and with their return a period of disgraceful persecution set in. "An arrogance of power" writes C. M. Andrews in *Colonial Self-Government, American Nation, Vol. V*, "seemed to possess the colony, and intolerance that brooked no check or control. The government of 'godly men' was in its way as tyrannical as ever had been, or was to be, the government of a Stuart."

THE HANGING OF MARY DYER

Four of the Quakers were hanged on Boston Common in 1660, among them Mary Dyer, the wife of the Secretary of Rhode Island, who had returned to Boston, whence she had been banished, after being whipped on her bare back through the streets of the city, tied behind a cart.

These executions, however, only served to increase the number of converts. Soon Charles II took notice of the cruelty of the

A Quaker Exhorter in New England

Illustration from
THE SECOND GENERATION OF ENGLISHMEN IN AMERICA
by Thomas Wentworth Higginson

Originally published in
HARPER'S MAGAZINE, *July,* 1883

Massachusetts authorities and he sent an order to Governor Endicott to stop them and to send the accused persons to England for trial. When a banished Quaker, bearing the king's order, appeared before Endicott with his hat on, the governor was so incensed that he was about to send him to jail; but when the Quaker handed Endicott the order from the throne, Endicott, himself thunderstruck, removed his own hat in deference to the presence of the king's messenger. Fearing to allow such bitter witnesses against their authority to testify before the king, the Boston rulers, instead of sending the accused persons to England, a thing they would never do in any event, immediately ordered the keeper of the Boston jail to set all the Quakers free. This ended the severe persecution of the Quakers in New England. The people of Massachusetts never had approved this severity against them, and finally public opinion, revolting at the acts of the ruling men, forced a repeal of the law of banishment against the sect. And so the martyrs had not died in vain. They had won a victory for members of their religious sect not only, but at the same time probably did a greater deed for Massachusetts itself by breaking down the exclusive religious policy that had prevailed in the colony up to this time. Thereafter, persons holding religious opinions and beliefs differing from that of the Boston church, though considered heretics by the Puritans, were nevertheless allowed to come and live in Massachusetts. Thus it was that Massachusetts was emancipated.

Mary Dyer on Her Way to the Scaffold

*With head erect, preceded and followed by drummers,
Mary Dyer marched from the jail to the place of execution
on Boston Common.   As she passed, the multitude which
lined the way stood hushed, awed by her saintly mien, from
which shone the spiritual light of the soul of the martyr.*

Illustration from
THE HANGING OF MARY DYER
by Basil King

Originally published in
McCLURE'S MAGAZINE, *November,* 1906

Chapter III

EVENTFUL YEARS IN COLONIAL HISTORY

SIR WILLIAM BERKELEY SURRENDERS TO THE COMMISSIONERS OF THE COMMONWEALTH

OING to Jamestown in 1660, the year in which Charles II began his reign, one would have witnessed great rejoicing there, for, of all the English colonies in America, no other had been so loyal to the Stuarts as Virginia. The years immediately following the execution of Charles I had witnessed the flocking to Virginia of large numbers of those devoted gentlemen known as Cavaliers, who had been the stanch partisans of Charles in his contest with Parliament. Most prominent among these believers in divine right was Sir William Berkeley, the then royalist governor of the colony, who had been chosen in 1642. At the impious deed of treason which the Puritans had committed against their sovereign he had stood aghast, and was at first for preserving Virginia for the martyred king's son. He blustered about and talked of resistance for a time, even making preparations for defense and managing to be the last territory belonging to England to submit to the republicans. Yet even this brave aristocrat saw that he could not count upon the united support of the colony, and so quickly surrendered to the commission sent with a strong fleet by Parliament in 1651 to reduce the Virginians to submission.

His retirement had lasted eight long years; the fall of the Commonwealth and the restoration of the monarchy in 1660 were, therefore, received in Virginia with a blaze of exultation on the part of the Cavaliers, and to commemorate the event, which the Virginians then deemed so happy, Sir William was once more called to Jamestown to be governor. Little, however, did the Virginians imagine, at this happy time, of the dire things that were to come to pass within a few short years, under the rule of this former gracious and affable gentleman. Whether it was the many toasts that he had drunk to King Charles during the days of his retirement, while the Commonwealth lasted, or whether it was his visit to England made in 1661, upon his return the next year, it was found that he had become, according to Wilson, "not a Virginian, like the chief Cavalier gentlemen about him, who now accounted Virginia their home and neighborhood, but a harsh and arbitrary servant of the crown and of his own interests, ready to fall into a rage at the slightest contradiction, suave only when he meant to strike."

His return from England occurring two years after the beginning of the reign of Charles II, in 1660—the year in which the Navigation Act of 1651 was put in operation and a second Navigation Act, placing even more restrictions on the trade of the colonies, was passed—it was natural that the House of Burgesses chosen in that year of royal jubilation would contain a large number of hearty supporters of the king's government, over whom Sir William would become the ruling spirit. At any rate, it happened that he was able through his own friends on the Council to run things pretty much his own way, and to obtain complete control of a legislature whose life he contrived to prolong for fifteen years, until 1676, simply by adjourning its sessions from year to year, and so having no elections at all. Having no sympathy with common people, whose representatives he thus succeeded in keeping out of the legislature, it was useless for the people to appeal to the House of Burgesses for

Sir William Berkeley Surrendering to the
Commissioners of the Commonwealth

Illustration from
IN WASHINGTON'S DAY
by Woodrow Wilson

Originally published in
HARPER'S MAGAZINE, *January,* 1896

[33]

a redress of their grievances. Deprived even of the very forms of their liberty, oppressed with heavy taxes which it was next to impossible for the small planters to pay, because the Navigation Act, by putting such restrictions on their carrying trade, made tobacco, which was the circulating medium in Virginia, worth very little and the goods it was to pay for worth very much, it became a difficult matter to live at all, "and," writes Wilson, "poverty seemed a thing enacted and enforced." Finally, in 1667, when the price of tobacco fell to a halfpenny a pound, Mr. Ludwell declared to the governor that only "faith in the mercy of God, loyalty to the king, and affection for the government" kept them from rising in rebellion.

As if these troubles were not enough, in 1672, says C. M. Andrews in *Colonial Self-Government*, "Charles II granted the whole of Virginia for thirty-one years to his friends and advisers, Arlington and Culpeper, and erected it into a proprietary province similar to that of Maryland. The powers of the grantees were to be those of a feudal lord, and many of the political privileges which the colony possessed were in danger of destruction." Protest was made against this usurpation, until a renunciation of the grant was obtained, the grantees retaining, however, the quit rents and escheats, in spite of all opposition. "And then, in 1675," to quote again from Wilson's *History of the American People*, "when affairs seemed most darkened and confused by selfish and arbitrary action both at home and oversea, there came hot trouble with the Indians which the governor refused either to deal with himself or allow others to settle.

BACON'S REBELLION

"It was that that brought the explosion. A sort of desperate wrath took possession of the stronger and more daring spirits of the colony, and they presently found a leader who gave Sir William good cause to fear what might come of their anger. The governor ought to have remembered that other year of blood, 1644, when last the Indians were on the warpath, and how sad a blow it had dealt the colony. True, there had then been scarcely ten thousand

[34]

A Virginia Plantation Wharf

Illustration from
IN WASHINGTON'S DAY
by Woodrow Wilson

Originally published in
HARPER'S MAGAZINE, *January,* 1896

people in Virginia, and there were now, no doubt, close upon fifty thousand, armed and able in all ordinary straits to take care of themselves. It was not likely the Indians could strike very far within the borders or threaten the heart of the colony. But men and women and children lived on the borders no less than at the heart of the colony. Precious lives could be wasted there as well as elsewhere—plain people, no doubt, but Englishmen—and the colonists were not likely to stand tamely by and look on at the massacre of their own people. No doubt the Indians had been unwisely, unjustly dealt with and provoked, goaded to hostile acts by attacks upon one tribe for what, it may be, another had done; such things had too often happened, and the colonists were not overcareful to avoid them. But that was no reason for refusing to put a force into the field to stop the massacres. What was the governor's scruple? He alone could grant licenses to trade with the Indians, and he did not grant them for nothing. It was something more than a surmise that he shared the profits of the trade and let the traders sell what they would to the savages, though it were firearms and powder and shot, against the laws of the colony, to make the profits worth while. Did he hesitate to interrupt his lucrative fur trade with the red men, or was he reluctant to put any armed force into the field for fear of what it might do for the redress of grievances within the colony after the danger from the Indians had been made an end of? Whatever his motive, he would not act, and could not, he said, until the Assembly came together for its regular meeting in March, 1676. Meanwhile scores of people had been murdered, plantation after plantation had been destroyed (sixty in a single county within a space of little more than two weeks), and the border was desolate and terror-stricken. And even when March came and the meeting of the burgesses, Berkeley played them false. The Assembly met, the 'Long Assembly' elected fifteen years ago, met for the last time, as it turned out—and voted to send a force of five hundred men against the savages; but Berkeley disbanded the little army before it could take the field; and defense was again abandoned.

A Virginia Planter in Retirement on His Estate

Illustration from
IN WASHINGTON'S DAY
by Woodrow Wilson

Originally published in
HARPER'S MAGAZINE, *January,* 1896

"Here was more than could be endured; and there were men in Virginia who were ready to defy the governor and get their rights by arms. Nathaniel Bacon had sworn with a hot oath that if the redskins meddled with him he would harry them, commission or no commission; and he kept his threat. He was of the hot blood that dares a great independence. He was great-grandson of Sir Thomas Bacon of Friston Hall, Suffolk, cousin to the great Lord Bacon, of whose fame the world had been full these fifty years; and though he was but nine-and-twenty, study at the Inns of Court and much travel in foreign lands had added to his gentle breeding the popular manners and the easy self-confidence of a man of the world before he turned his back upon England and came with his young wife to be a planter on James River in Virginia. In May news came that the Indians had attacked his own upper plantation and had murdered his overseer and one of his favorite servants; and he did not hesitate what to do. A company of armed and mounted men begged him to go with them against the redskins, and he led them forth upon their bloody errand without law or license, member of the governor's Council and magistrate though he was. He sent to ask the governor for a commission, indeed, but he did not turn back, or lose his armed following, either, when word was brought that the governor had refused it and had proclaimed him and all with him to be outlaws. It was flat rebellion; but Bacon's pulse only quickened at that, and Virginia for a little while seemed his to command.

"He put a stirring tragedy upon the stage there in the quiet colony with its somber forests, and played it out with a dash and daring that must take every generous man's imagination who remembers how fair and winning a figure the young leader made through all those uneasy days, and how irresistibly he caught the eye and the fancy with the proud way in which he carried himself, lithe and tall and dark of skin, and that melancholy light in his dusky eye, a man of action and of passion—such passion as it moves and wins other men to look upon. That was a summer to be remembered, in which he pushed to the front in affairs—and most of all its sad ending.

[38]

On The Warpath

Illustration from
COLONIES AND NATION
by Woodrow Wilson

Originally published in
HARPER'S MAGAZINE, *March*, 1901

"Berkeley found that he could not openly treat Bacon as a rebel without kindling a flame of discontent on every hand among the colonists. He was obliged to dissolve the 'Long Assembly,' call a new one, admit Bacon himself to a seat in it, hear his bad administration debated, and consent at last to the levying of an effective force to fight the Indians. But what he could not do openly he tried to do secretly and by treachery. One night while the Assembly still sat Nathaniel Bacon fled from Jamestown, warned that his life was in danger. He returned with six hundred men at his back and compelled the governor to give him a commission. Once more he was proclaimed an outlaw, and all his followers outlaws with him, the moment he had turned his back and plunged into the Indian country; and a war for protection turned to civil war.

THE BURNING OF JAMESTOWN

"Bacon's blows were quick and terrible, and more to be feared than his biting speech. He had well-nigh exterminated the Indian tribe of Susquehannocks before he heard of or heeded his outlawry. Then he turned in his hot anger against the government itself, as if it had declared war upon him. He required and took of his followers an oath to resist not only the governor, but the very troops of the king himself, should they come, until wrongs should be righted; and Berkeley was driven, a fugitive, to the far counties beyond the bay. When he returned with a motley force to Jamestown he was driven forth again, and Jamestown was burned. Only Bacon's death ended the ugly business. As autumn approached he sickened and died (the first day of October, 1676), overcome by the passion of action and of feeling, and the exhausting life of the camp and the field; and his followers dispersed.

"He had gone too far. At first, rank and file, no doubt, had been with him, men of substance with the rest, for the right to live and to better the government; but most of the chief planters had held aloof even then; and as he went on they were more and more alienated. It became more and more an affair of the rabble, of the men who were poor and desperate and had nothing to lose. When

The Burning of Jamestown

Illustration from
COLONIES AND NATION
by Woodrow Wilson

Originally published in
HARPER'S MAGAZINE, *March,* 1901

he burned Jamestown he also sacked the plantations of the greater landowners thereabouts, knowing them to be his enemies; and he died with the spirit of the outlaw too much kindled within him by the lawless work he had done, almost determined to withstand the king as well as the governor, and to make those who had not joined him pay for his work of resistance and reform—no longer merely a champion of reasonable reformation, but a revolutionist. Nothing less could have alienated his friends, broken his party, and given Berkeley his full time of revenge against those whose cause had been just.

"That revenge was only too complete. A fleet arrived out of England in January, 1677, with a regiment of the king's troops aboard, and commissioners to settle the troubles in the colony to the re-establishing of order; and the commissioners had themselves to rebuke and restrain the insensate bitterness of the maddened governor. He had set the hangman to work before they came, and by the time January was out had sent more than twenty persons to the gallows for their participation in the rebellion; among the rest William Drummond, the capable Scotsman whom he had deputed to be the first governor of the settlements at Albemarle, and who had governed very quietly there, knowing the men he had to deal with, but who was now in Virginia again, Mr. Bacon's friend and counselor. 'As I live,' cried the king, when he learned the news from Virginia, 'the old fool has put to death more people in that naked country than I did for the murder of my father'; and he showed little patience when the old man came home to make his peace. The king would not see him, and the broken governor was dead—of chagrin, men said—by midsummer (1677). Virginia was rid of him; forgot how well she had liked him at first; and remembered without compunction how her people had celebrated his departure with bonfires and the booming of cannon."

LOADING SHIPS IN ALBEMARLE SOUND

In this memorable year of Bacon's Rebellion, troubles also broke out in the territory called Albemarle, a district in the northern part of North Carolina to the south of Virginia, where a settlement

From *Harper's Magazine*, March, 1901
LOADING SHIPS IN ALBEMARLE SOUND

had been made by colonists from Virginia and some traders from New England shortly after Charles II came to the throne—the first permanent settlement to be made in this region since the disastrous attempt by Raleigh in 1584.

Though not exactly neglected by the proprietors, the settlement did not receive much help from them. The people depended for a livelihood upon the cultivation of the soil, and the export of furs and tobacco, which they shipped in vessels from New England; and when their trade with New England was cut off by the enforce-

[43]

ment of the Navigation Acts, and poverty threatened them, they rose against the authorities and governed themselves for two years, in a manner that would have pleased Mr. Bacon himself.

"William Drummond," writes Wilson, "who had lived among them, had led Mr. Bacon to hope, and half expect, that these Albemarle men would send him aid and make common cause with him against the power of a royal governor and rich landowners; but they had saved their struggle for themselves. They took little thought for Virginia, and they could not have helped Mr. Bacon to succeed had they wished to help him. He had rebelled against powers which were already firmly established and which were to dominate Virginia throughout all the rest of her youth and of her growth to maturity." There were at this time in Virginia many men of wealth—the rich planters whom we would call "country gentlemen," and although many of them sympathized with Mr. Bacon in his protest against the oligarchical rule of Berkeley and the enforcement of the Navigation Acts, yet when it came to open rebellion these men would not follow.

"It was not this government of the 'country gentlemen,' at any rate," continues Wilson, "that had brought on the fatal troubles with the redskins which had stirred Mr. Bacon to his first act of rebellion; for New England also, self-governed and free as yet, had had her own struggle with the Indians, even more terrible and bitter, which had ended that same eventful summer of 1676. The New England Indians had not forgotten the fate of the Pequots; but that was now close upon forty years ago; the terror of it was no longer fresh, and their own situation had meantime grown a bit desperate. They were being shut within intolerably narrow bounds, and they could not move away from the regions where the English were slowly crowding them from their hunting grounds without invading the territory of other tribes who would have no welcome for them. The white men paid for the lands they took, but they did not permit the red men to refuse to sell. They played the part of masters always, and there could be no hope of better times to come. Devoted missionaries had come among the tribes from the white

Death of Indian Chief Alexander, Brother of
King Philip

Illustration from
AN INDIAN JOURNEY
by Lucy C. Lillie

Originally published in
HARPER'S MAGAZINE, *November,* 1885

settlements and had won many of them to believe in the gospel of the true God, but their preaching was like the telling of idle fables to most of the reticent, intractable people of the forest, and left them untouched. They were ready at last when a leader should arise to plot for an uprising and a last trial of strength with the invading palefaces. Such a leader arose in the person of Philip, the chief of the Wampanoags, whom the English had penned up within the narrow peninsula of Good Hope by the Bay of Narragansett."

DEATH OF THE INDIAN CHIEF ALEXANDER

Some six years before, the Plymouth people heard rumors that Philip and his elder brother, Alexander, who had succeeded his father, Massasoit, as chief of the Wampanoags, were only too anxious for war. Chief Alexander was especially under suspicion of being in league with the Narragansetts, and Governor Winslow ordered his arrest. To be taken captive to Plymouth fairly broke this proud Indian's heart. On his way home he was taken suddenly ill and in a few hours was dead. His young wife, Wetamoo, was most bitter and vindictive against her husband's captors, and when she saw him dead her anger knew no bounds, for she believed he had been poisoned by the English. The dead chief was taken upon a litter and carried to the banks of the river. Placing the body on a grassy mound beneath a majestic tree, the warriors gathered around in silence to witness the departure of his spirit to the realms of the red man's immortality.

The death of his brother soured the mind of Philip toward the English, and he now began to scheme and plot in earnest to obtain revenge. "The flame which Philip kindled among the Wampanoags," as described by Wilson, "promptly spread to the Narragansetts and the Nipmucks, until it burned on every border, and New England saw a day of terror such as she had never seen before. There was no trouble like Virginia's. No governor hesitated, no armed force lacked authority to do its work of protection and attack, no levy lagged or was tardy; the country rallied to the awful business. The fatal uprising began in June, 1675, and was ended—for

those tribes, at least—by August, 1676, as the Pequot war had
ended, with the annihilation of the offending tribes. Those that

From *Harper's Magazine*, June, 1883
THE DEATH OF KING PHILIP

were not killed or taken were driven forth in hopeless flight; those
that were taken were sold as slaves in the West Indies."

[47]

THE DEATH OF KING PHILIP

King Philip himself, driven to his last place of refuge at Mount Hope, was surrounded by men under Capt. Ben Church of Plymouth and shot by an Indian of Church's party, whose brother Philip had killed for counseling submission to the English. "Thereafter," says Wilson, "there were only the tribes in the north to reckon with. But the white men's loss was almost as great as that of the savages. More than one-half of the towns of Massachusetts and Plymouth had seen the torch and the tomahawk that awful year; twelve of them had been utterly destroyed; no fewer than six hundred buildings, chiefly dwellings, had been burned; six hundred men had lost their lives, and scores of women and children; debts had been piled up and damage suffered which it would take years of bitter toil to pay and repair; and New England was for a little like a place desolate and stricken. But she rallied in time, as always before, and slowly worked her way to better days, like the old days for peace and prosperity. Her dangers and anxieties were, at any rate, lessened in one matter that had often seemed to hold fear and danger permanently at its heart."

Chapter IV

THE DUTCH FOUNDING OF NEW YORK

THE years that had been so eventful in the history of Virginia and Massachusetts were to be more important in the annals of New Netherland, which the Dutch had first settled in 1626 when Peter Minuit purchased, on behalf of the Dutch West India Company, the entire island of Manhattan from the Indians for twenty-four dollars.

ALONG THE CANAL IN OLD MANHATTAN

At the time of this first settlement many of the colonists of the Dutch West India Company had misgivings about settling at the southern end of the island, feeling that this location would render the settlement too easy of attack by the English sea rovers who at that period were pushing their expeditions in all directions. Besides, it was known that England claimed this whole territory by virtue of the charter granted to the Virginia and Plymouth Companies. And so they were for pitching their tents at Spuyten Duyvil; there they had found lovely meadow lands with running water, affording an excellent opportunity to dig and equip canals, and, besides, the site was so shut in by adjacent hills as to be hidden from the eyes of foreign adventurers, whom they feared might find entrance to the harbor below. But an appeal to national pride and wiser counsels prevailed and it was finally resolved to begin operations at the point which is now the Battery. And all opposition was silenced as soon as it was demonstrated that a canal could be dug at once, running through what is now Broad Street. This at once lent the charm of home to the chosen site, and all was peace.

"Actually," writes Thomas A. Janvier in *Old New York*, "only two roads were established when the town of New Amsterdam was founded, and these so obviously were necessary that, practically, they established themselves. One of them, on line of the present Stone and Pearl Streets—the latter then the waterfront—led from the Fort to the Brooklyn ferry at about the present Peck Slip. The other, on the line of the present Broadway, led northward from the Fort, past farms and gardens falling away toward the North River, as far as the present Park Row; and along the line of that street, and of Chatham Street, and of the Bowery, went on into the wilderness. After the palisade was erected, this road was known as far as the city gate (at Wall Street) as the Heere Straat, or High Street; and beyond the wall as the Heere Wegh—for more than a century the only highway that traversed the island from end to end.

"Broad Street and the Beaver's Path primarily were not streets at all. On the line of the first of these, with a roadway on each side, a canal extended as far as Beaver Street; where it narrowed to a ditch which drained the swamp that extended northward to about the present Exchange Place. On the line of the Beaver's Path, east and west from the main ditch, were lateral ditches at the lower end of the swamp. This system of surface drainage having converted the swamp into a meadow, it became known as the Sheep Pasture. Down beneath the modern surface the ancient swamp remains to this present day.

"Because of the homelikeness—as one sat contentedly smoking on one's stoop in the cool of summer evenings—that there was in having a good strong-smelling canal under one's nose, and pleasant sight of round, squat sailormen aboard of boats which also were of a squat roundness, Broad Street (then called the Heere Graft) was a favorite dwelling place with the quality of that early day; and even the Beaver's Path—which could boast only a minor, ditchlike smell, that yet was fit to bring tears of homesickness into one's eyes, such tender associations did it arouse—was well thought of by folk of the humbler sort, to whom the smell of a whole canal was too great a luxury."

Minuit with a council of five as "Director General" governed

[50]

Along the Canal in Old Manhattan

Illustration from
THE EVOLUTION OF NEW YORK
by Thomas A. Janvier

Originally published in
HARPER'S MAGAZINE, *May,* 1893

the Colony for the company in Holland. But during the five years of his rule, not many colonists came, and in 1629 the West India Company attempted to attract settlers by establishing the so-called patroon system, by which members of the company, who would bring at their own expense at least fifty colonists to New Netherland, would be granted an extensive tract of land along the Hudson River. With the grant went all feudal rights, which gave the patroons full jurisdiction over the tenants on the land, also full liberty to trade, subject to the company's regulations. The patroons soon became great landowners, many of them combining their holdings by partnerships, and thus absorbing the trade over which the company claimed a monopoly. The company would not tolerate this. Minuit, thought to favor the patroons, was therefore replaced by Wouter Van Twiller. But his selection was unfortunate, and after a misrule of five years, during which he enriched himself at the company's expense, he was removed in 1637.

In the year 1638 there came to New Amsterdam to replace Van Twiller "a brisk, waspish little old gentleman," universally known as "William the Testy." Broad was his face and sharp were his features; "and his cheeks were scorched into a dusky red" by his "two fierce little gray eyes," while "the corners of his mouth were modeled into a kind of fretwork" resembling the muzzle "of an irritable pug dog." Such is the description of William Kieft, the new Director-General, as given by Irving in *Knickerbocker's History of New York*, and adds, "he was one of the most positive, restless, ugly little men that ever put himself in a passion about nothing." One would expect a man of this character to raise Cain, and, sure enough, his rule was autocratic and tyrannical and brought all sorts of troubles upon New Netherland. There were quarrels with the Swedes on the Delaware; quarrels with the English in Connecticut, but, worst of all, Kieft involved the colony in a disastrous conflict with the Indians, who threatened the very existence of the colony until they were finally quelled by the military skill of Capt. John Underhill of New England.

The effects of this terrible Indian war and the continued

"Some of the Bystanders Said: 'She is drunk.
It will soon pass away.'"

Illustration from
NEW YORK SLAVE TRADERS
by Thomas A. Janvier
Originally published in
HARPER'S MAGAZINE, *January,* 1895

despotic rule of Kieft finally led his chosen advisers to complain to the company, and their petition for a new governor was granted.

In 1639 the patroon system was modified; the policy of monopoly as to trade and land ownership was abandoned. The right to occupy and cultivate land upon the payment of an annual rent was now open to all comers, as was likewise the trade of the colony. This change in policy resulted in a great influx of settlers—English as well as Dutch, and many Virginians came to engage in tobacco culture. By the year 1664 New Amsterdam, destined to become the metropolis of the New World, had grown to be a substantial town of sixteen hundred and sixty inhabitants, while the total population of the province of New Netherland was about ten thousand. In the city itself, where the Hollanders predominated, the Dutch spirit was fully developed.

THE DUTCH SLAVE TRADERS

That the Dutch merchants of New Amsterdam considered slave dealing a respectable industry not only, but a most profitable kind of maritime adventure, will be shown in the following story taken from Thomas A. Janvier's "New York Slave Traders," published in *Harper's Magazine* for January, 1895:

"From the very foundation of the New Netherland colony slavery was part and parcel of its economic organization. Under the conditions then existing this was a matter of necessity. A colonial establishment of that period, to be well equipped, required slaves in just the same way that it required horses and cows. . . . The Dutch in New Netherland did succeed in making slaves of a few Indians, but these creatures were of so perverse a disposition that using them on a large scale was impossible. Therefore—the matter being facilitated by the possession by the Dutch West India Company of trading stations on the African coast—the New-Netherlanders drew from Africa, either directly or by way of the Dutch West Indies, their necessary supply of beasts of toil.

"So normal an institution was slavery in those days . . . that I cannot determine from the records when slave holding on this

The Choicest Pieces of her Cargo Were
Sold at Auction

Illustration from
NEW YORK SLAVE TRADERS
by Thomas A. Janvier
Originally published in
HARPER'S MAGAZINE, *January,* 1895

island began. The first formal mention of it is in the Charter of Liberties and Exemptions of 1629, the thirtieth clause of which instrument declares that 'The Company will use their endeavors to supply the colonists with as many blacks as they conveniently can, on the conditions hereafter to be made'; and in the New Project of Liberties and Exemptions, the thirty-first clause provides that 'in like manner the Incorporated West India Company shall allot to each Patroon twelve black men and women, out of the prizes in which Negroes shall be found, for the advancement of the Colonies in New Netherland.'"

Other testimony could be quoted to show "that slavery on this island practically was contemporaneous with the establishment in possession here of the Dutch West India Company that, practically, it was a cardinal characteristic of the town of New Amsterdam—which was to be in the fullness of time the city of New York—from the very start.

"Actually, in those early days of the colony, the number of slaves in New Netherland was small. The promise of the West India Company to provide blacks for the colonists was so conditioned that it amounted to little; and at the same time the company's laws forbade the dispatch of slave ships direct to Africa by the colonists themselves. Yet the need for laborers in the colony was very urgent indeed."

In order, therefore, that New Netherland "might be adequately supplied with laborers, and that the slave trade which hath so long lain dormant to the great damage of the company, might by degrees be again revived," the company determined "to give the colonists a chance to try what they could do in the slave trade for themselves—which permission was accorded under date of April 4, 1652, with the limitations that the New York ships should not trade to the eastward of Popo (that they might be kept at a safe distance from the Gold Coast), and that a duty of fifteen guilders should be paid precedent to the landing in America of each slave." The first action taken under this act seems to have occurred in November, 1654, when "appeared before the Directors Jan de

Along the Water Front in Old New York

Illustration from
THE EVOLUTION OF NEW YORK
by Thomas A. Janvier

Originally published in
HARPER'S MAGAZINE, *May,* 1893

Sweerts and Dirck Pietersen and asked liberty to sail with their vessel the *White Horse* to the coast of Africa to obtain a cargo of slaves and to import the same to New Netherland. . . .

THE CHOICEST PIECES OF HER CARGO WERE SOLD AT AUCTION

"The *White Horse*, presumably the first slave ship, properly so called, that ever entered this harbor, arrived in the late spring or early summer of the year 1655; and the choicest pieces of her cargo, sold at auction, fetched about one hundred and twenty-five dollars each. . . . Yet were some of these purchases very bad investments indeed. When the sale was no more than ended several of the negroes 'were found to have been infected with some fatal disorder'; of which the first case to declare itself was that of a girl bought by Nicholas Boot, 'whilst being led home along the shore of the East River, being opposite to Litschoe's tavern, she fell, crying, "Ariba!" She was taken up and, proceeding a few paces farther, again fell, her eyes being fixed in her head. Her owner coming up asked what was the matter? Upon which she cried, "Moa! Moa!" Some of the bystanders said: "She is drunk. It will soon pass away. She is sound at heart." At the city gate she was put in a wagon and taken to her master's house, but died in the evening.'

ON THE WATER FRONT IN OLD NEW YORK

"It was on what now is Pearl Street, then the water front, and —as is shown by the reference to Litschoe's tavern and to the city gate—a little to the south of what now is Wall Street, that this poor purchase of Nicholas Boot's fell down a-dying; a tragedy not easily reconstructed mentally nowadays in the dingy thoroughfare in the twilight beneath the Elevated Railway and to the clanging accompaniment of rushing trains."

Whether or not other private ventures followed that of the *White Horse*, it is certain that the West India Company took the trade presently into their own hands, as we learn that the vessel *Oak Tree* sailed in the company's name, from New Amsterdam to the coast of Africa in the year 1659. . . .

"WE ESCAPED IN THE BOAT"

"The result of the venture in the *Oak Tree* is hidden away at Amsterdam in the manuscript archives of the West India Company; but there survives more openly, in the printed records, the log of another ship belonging to the company, the *St. John*, which made a voyage to Africa under a like charter in the same year, 1659.

"In its earlier portion this record is typical, no doubt, of the ordinary experience at that time of slaves on the West African coast. The *St. John* traded successfully at 'Rio Real, before a village named Bavy,' where were taken on board 'two hundred and nineteen slaves, men, women, boys, and girls'; which number was increased to three hundred and ninety in the course of farther trade at 'Rio Camerones' and at other points along the coast. But even while this good trading was going on, difficulty was encountered in procuring food; and then, presently, 'by reason of the excessive rains' and 'through the bad victuals with which we were provided at Delmina' (the Elmira of the present day) 'many of our slaves were affected by a malignant dysentery. . . .' In some way or another the run of eleven weeks across the Atlantic was accomplished with no further misfortune, saving, of course, the steady diminution of the cargo by death. . . . And then, at last, being come almost to the destined port, the log records: 'On the 1st November, two hours before daylight, lost the ship on the Rocks of Rocus, and we escaped in the boat to the island of Curaçoa, leaving in the ship eighty-five slaves—as there was no hope of saving the slaves when we were compelled to leave the vessel in the heavy surge.'

"In the end, the slaves actually were saved, but not in a way profitable to the company," for the barque *Young Spotted Cow* sent by the company to salvage the wreck, owing to the high seas, did not succeed in fastening the hawser to the wreck, and, while awaiting the assistance of another company's vessel, an English privateer appeared and captured the *Young Spotted Cow* and, "having transferred eighty-four slaves to her, sent her toward the continent. . . .

"But even a total loss now and then, and the considerable loss by death which was a constant factor in the trade, mattered little—

when the profits as a whole were so refreshingly large that every shareholder rubbed together his big hands comfortably as he pocketed the annual dividends which the company declared. As against this total loss just recorded, Mr. Vice-Director Beck, at Curaçoa, wrote to Mr. Director-General Stuyvesant, at New Amsterdam, in August, 1659, 'The company's ship *King Solomon* arrived here on the 2nd July from Guinea with three hundred and thirty-one slaves, of which I sold three hundred for cash to a certain Spanish merchant to be paid on delivery.' And the vice-director, pleasantly elated by his good stroke of business, continues: 'I expect every day a ship with negroes; and I wish they were arrived here, even if they were a thousand in number, as I expect the return of the aforesaid merchant to take with him all, as he is able and willing to do.'

"In this same letter the vice-director adds: 'From the aforesaid negroes Frank Bruyn selected for Your Honor two boys and a girl, who are conveyed in the same vessel that bears this. I endeavored as much as possible to secure them from the cold. Frank Bruyn also made a purchase of two others for the Commissary Van Bruggh, who are also shipped by this opportunity. The Commissary Laurens Van Ruyven also bought here two young negroes on account of his brother, the Secretary in New Netherland. A similar parcel was sold here at one hundred and fifty dollars.'

"There was trouble over this consignment when it arrived at New Amsterdam, partly arising from Mr. Commissary Van Bruggh's selfishness, and partly from the inconsiderate manner in which one of the five head of negroes died on the passage—and so confused the vice-director's, the commissary's and the director-general's joint accounts. In the ensuing February the director-general wrote to the vice-director: 'To avoid dispute, I left, for this time, the choice to the commissary, who took one black girl and one of the stoutest boys. But even this is not without difficulty, as one of the five died in coming hither, others fell sick on the voyage or shortly after their arrival, from which the difficulty in settling the account arises. To prevent which in future the negroes ought to be

"We Escaped in the Boat"

Illustration from
NEW YORK SLAVE TRADERS
by Thomas A. Janvier

Originally published in
HARPER'S MAGAZINE, *January*, 1895

designated by the seller by some name or mark.' And again, six months later, his suggestion not having been heeded, the governor wrote: 'Referring to the negroes recently arrived by the ship *Indian*, we recommend you that if hereafter negroes be sent by one vessel, some for individuals and some for the company, they be marked by particular signs, either with a string in their clothes or some other manner, so that disputes may be prevented; inasmuch as during the voyage of the *Indian* some few of the slaves fell sick and died.'

"The last Dutch slaver to enter this port before New Amsterdam fell into the hands of the English was the ship *Gideon*. Under date of October 23, 1663, 'the commissioners and directors for the management of the South (Delaware) River in New Netherland' expressed themselves to the directors of the West India Company as 'of the opinion, under direction,' that at least fifty negroes should be sent to that region immediately. . . ."

This suggestion went over the seas to the directors in Holland, who, in the easy-going, slow Dutch way, finally saw the wisdom of it and "in due season word was dispatched to Governor Stuyvesant that a contract had been made with one Symen Gilde, master of the ship *Gideon*, to 'take in a good cargo of slaves at Loango,' and to proceed thence, via Curaçoa, to New Amsterdam—whence the slaves needed for the South River were to be forwarded and the remainder were to be sold on the company's account.

"Thus gently advancing, the project of the South River Commissioners did at last materialize; and on the 17th of August, 1664, Governor Stuyvesant sent down to them, by 'a Savage who carries it by Land,' a letter in which was the announcement: 'There arrived here in safety, God be praised, on the 15th inst., the ship *Gideon*, which left Curaçoa on the 21st July, with 300 slaves, *vizt* 160 males and 140 females, of whom 9 died during the passage; the whole being a poor assortment.' Yet would it have been better for the South River people had the march of events in this matter exhibited a little more celerity—inasmuch as, only nine days after the Governor had dispatched his letter by the land-traveling savage, there came sailing up through the Narrows that English fleet which was to pounce upon slaves and masters together, and at a stroke was to change the Dutch province of New Netherland into the English province of New York. . . ."

ARRIVAL OF STUYVESANT AT NEW AMSTERDAM, 1647

But to return to our story, Peter Stuyvesant, who replaced the obnoxious Kieft, and destined to be the last Dutch governor of New York, was born in Holland in 1602. He was a brave soldier in the Dutch military service in the West Indies, and was director or governor of the colony of Curaçoa. He was a remarkably strongheaded official. He had lost a leg in battle in the West Indies, and, with a wooden one, bound with silver bands, he came to New Netherland as its governor late in May, 1647. He was received with joy as the successor of Kieft. He assumed great dignity, marched from the vessel to the Fort with great pomp, and assured the people that justice should rule. He began his administration by the assertion of viceregal authority, and frowned upon every expression of republican sentiment, declaring it to be treason to petition against one's magistrate, "whether there be cause

DUTCH SOLDIER
From Mural Decoration, Hudson County Court House, Jersey City, New Jersey

or not." He defended Kieft's conduct in rejecting the interference of the council of the twelve, saying, "If any one, during my administration, shall appeal, I will make him a foot shorter, and send the pieces to Holland, and let him appeal in that way."

"According to his lights (which were few) and within his limitations (which were many) Stuyvesant," says Thomas A. Janvier in his *Dutch Founding of New York*, "was in the way of becoming a reformer: and reformers ever have been painted blackest by those whom they sought to reform. That outrageous little colony needed a deal of reforming when he took over the government: and had his mandatory proclamation stopped with the one that forbade 'Sabbath breaking, brawling, and drunkenness,' he still would have had a hornets' nest about his ears. Not content with trying to reduce to decency the energetic social customs of the colonists, he tried also to bring them up to the line of honest dealing: and so struck at their pockets as well as at their hearts. He forbade the sale of liquor to the savages; a most profitable business in itself, and of much indirect advantage to those engaged in it—because an intoxicated savage obviously was more desirable than a sober savage to bargain with for furs. He made stringent regulations which checked the profitable industry of smuggling peltries into New England, and European goods thence into New Netherland. And on top of all this, further to replenish the exhausted treasury of the colony, he levied a tax upon liquors and wines. That was the climax of his offending. As the outraged and indignant colonists themselves declared—becomingly falling back upon Holy Writ for a strong enough simile—the wine and liquor tax was 'like the crowning of Rehoboam.'

"Under such a government as Stuyvesant gave to that unfortunate colony there could be no real improvement in its affairs. Even when his attempted reforms were sound—and for the most part they were sound—the effect of them was weakened, and their realization was made difficult or impossible, by the manner in which they were applied."

Arrival of Stuyvesant in New Amsterdam

Illustration from
COLONIES AND NATION
by Woodrow Wilson

Originally published in
HARPER'S MAGAZINE, *February,* 1901

At the beginning of Stuyvesant's administration his need of money forced him to establish a board of nine men who were to represent the people and confer with him on all matters concerning the city. But Director Stuyvesant in his own mind intended that these nine men would assist only when called upon, and "Czar" Peter resolved that this would be seldom. Quarrels resulted, and the end of the matter was the incorporation of New Amsterdam as a city in 1653.

Before the end of Stuyvesant's rule New Amsterdam had taken on that cosmopolitan character which has continued to distinguish it up to the present day. Representatives of various European nations began to flock to the city, until by 1655, it is said, more than fifteen different languages were spoken in its streets and taverns.

In the Dutch city of New Amsterdam the tavern from the very first was a place of great importance. With the increase in population and the many traders who came from New England and Virginia and other parts, it was necessary to provide more and better accommodations. So a stone structure was built by Kieft on Pearl Street, known as the City Tavern, which became the Stadt Huys, or City Hall, when the city was elevated into the dignity of a municipality in 1653. There were many other taverns, large and small, each with its tap room where the thirsty could quench their thirst. Then as in modern New York—at least until the days of prohibition—the city was noted for its beer and the great number of drinking places, which inclines one to believe that New-Yorkers were always fond of their schnapps.

A GAME OF BOWLS

The Dutch innkeepers made little or no distinction between their guests, for, since all paid alike, one guest was considered as good as another. Whoever came to such a house of entertainment must eat as others ate, drink as others drank, sit at table with the other guests, and go to bed when the company had done drinking. Thus, in a way, the innkeeper played the part of an autocrat.

[66]

A Game of Bowls

Illustration from
OLD NEW YORK TAVERNS
by John Austin Stevens
Originally published in
HARPER'S MAGAZINE, *May,* 1890

In the old Dutch days before the English came, the honest burgher was accustomed to spend the summer evenings beneath the low porch of his favorite inn. There in solid comfort he would smoke his long clay pipe and drink his schnapps, watching the

From *Harper's Magazine*, March, 1881

NEW YEAR'S HYMN TO ST. NICHOLAS

Among the Dutch Christmas was of little importance, New Year was the great day

while the quiet game of bowls upon the green hard by, with which every good tavern was equipped.

In this growing city of New Amsterdam the continued arbitrary rule of the hot-headed Peter had gained for him in 1653 the opposition of his own countrymen. Nor could he now, as heretofore, depend for support on the English residents within the colony, as the States-General of Holland had ordered that only Dutchmen should hold public office.

[68]

The Dutch Founding of New York

At this particular time England and Holland were fighting their first war over the Navigation Acts. Had not the declaration of peace in 1654 come just in time to prevent Cromwell's fleet under Major Sedgwick from leaving Boston harbor, the Dutch at New Amsterdam must surely have been beaten then and there.

But his English neighbors in Connecticut continued their gradual advance, and in 1662 they were claiming Westchester as well as the whole of Long Island, which caused the Director-General to realize that Dutch rule in America was nearing its end. Nor was he wrong in his surmise. As we shall see, the fate that

HENRY HUDSON AND THE HALF-MOON
From the Mural Decoration, Hudson County Court House, Jersey City, New Jersey

almost overtook him and New Netherland under the Commonwealth was to be consummated by Charles II, who had just recently been restored to the throne of his father.

This presentiment of disaster to himself and New Netherland was no delusion on the part of Stuyvesant. At this very time Charles II had decided that so rich a prize as New Netherland must be added to his dominions, and this at a time when both countries were at peace. Did not England own all the country along the American coast "from the French settlements in the north to Florida and the Spanish settlements in the south," by virtue of the charter granted to the London and Plymouth companies for the planting of colonies at Jamestown and Plymouth? And did not New Netherland, lying midway between New England and Virginia, likewise belong to the English crown? Was it not an Englishman, Henry Hudson, who, sailing in the *Half Moon*, discovered Hudson's River, and so brought the Dutch to Manhattan Island? The settlements made at New Netherland were considered by the English to be mere trading posts, and, though the Dutch were not molested there during forty years and more, the time had now come for England to take possession of its own, which the king said "did belong to England heretofore," but from which "the Dutch by degrees drove our people out." This claim of English ownership to the Dutch province was a mere pretext and had no justice in it; but principles of justice were little thought of by Charles II or those who governed for him. All they saw was the commercial supremacy of the Dutch; all they cared to know was that Dutch merchants were taking away the trade that should belong to England alone. They knew that the Dutch colony in America, through the key position of New Amsterdam, controlled the fur trade of the Five Nations, and that the Dutch frontiers were in almost direct contact with those of the French in the valley of the Ohio, the military command of which meant the control of the American continent. Thus situated between the English colonies in Virginia and New England, there was little hindrance to the planters and traders to sell tobacco contrary to the Navigation Acts and so defraud the king of his revenues.

It was obvious, therefore, that the Navigation Acts could not be enforced in America so long as "the English colonies had the Dutch next door to trade with as they pleased"; neither could England ever hope to control the heart of the American continent and the land of the fur trade while the Dutch were in control of Hudson's River.

Charles did not give the Dutch notice of his intentions by a declaration of war, but proceeded secretly with his plans for a surprise attack on New Amsterdam, lulling to rest the suspicions of Stuyvesant by giving out that the English fleet that set sail in June, 1664, was intended to investigate the condition of the New England colonies. But on this fleet of three ships of war were embarked four hundred and fifty soldiers under the command of

Richard Nichols, groom of the king's bedchamber, already appointed governor of the as yet unconquered province, together with

From *Harper's Magazine*, July, 1883

PETER STUYVESANT TEARING THE LETTER DEMANDING THE SURRENDER
OF NEW YORK

Colonels Cartwright and Carr, and Mr. Samuel Maverick, whose chief duties were to chastise Massachusetts, whose independent attitude the king did not like.

[71]

STUYVESANT TEARS UP LETTER DEMANDING SURRENDER

The entire territory of New Netherland was granted with full proprietary rights to the king's brother James, Duke of York; the fleet, with Nichols in command, was to take possession in the duke's name. As was expected, New Amsterdam, as Charles McLean Andrews relates in *Colonial Self-Government*, "fell an easy prey to the fleet. Stuyvesant wished to fight. When he received from Nichols the letter demanding the surrender of the city, he tore it in pieces

PETER STUYVESANT AND THE ENGLISH FLEET

and in a storm of wrath stamped on the torn fragments and declared to the members of the council that he would never yield. But the phlegmatic burghers refused to support him, and, gathering the pieces of the letter, they read the communication and answered it with a flag of truce. August 26, 1664, the English occupied the city. Nichols made every effort to conciliate the defeated burghers and to build up the colony, for by the terms of the capitulation the Dutch were allowed to remain in the colony if they chose, to have liberty of conscience and worship, to retain their own customs, and to enjoy all the privileges of English subjects."

The bloodless revolution by which New Amsterdam became New York and Fort Amsterdam became Fort James meant the annexation not only of a new province, but the control of the

[72]

American continent. Now possessed of the valley of Hudson's River and inheriting the Dutch friendship of the Five Nations, Champlain's attack on whom in 1608 had forever embittered them against the French, the English held such a strategic position in relation to the French in Canada, that the doom of New France in America, decreed for the next century, was already written.

During the four years of his governorship Nichols ruled the province under the duke's laws with fairness and wisdom, combined

FROM THE MURAL DECORATION, HUDSON COUNTY COURT HOUSE
JERSEY CITY, NEW JERSEY

with such tact that where strife had been so rife, all was now peace and harmony. His successor was Francis Lovelace, who also administered the province in fairness and justice during the four years of his governorship, which were rudely interrupted by the Dutch recapture of New York in July, 1673. But this occupation was a mere interlude in the history of the province, for by the Treaty of Westminster it was returned to Charles II and was formally surrendered to Edmund Andros upon his arrival in New York, October, 1674. Andros was to be the new governor, commissioned by the Duke of York to be his deputy in the government of New York "and its dependencies."

On the grounds that the Dutch occupation had annulled the Duke of York's title to New York given him in 1664, King Charles in 1674, to remove all doubt, made a brand-new grant of the province to his royal brother; and in turn James at once granted East New Jersey over again to Sir George Carteret, but without any mention of the right of sovereignty in the territory.

From *Harper's Magazine*, May, 1893

STUYVESANT SURRENDERING FORT AMSTERDAM TO THE ENGLISH

In August, 1665, when Nichols was governor of New York, Philip Carteret, the nephew of Sir George, with a company of colonists, made a settlement at Elizabethtown, and became the first governor of New Jersey. Andros, acting under the duke's instructions, and taking advantage of the death of Sir George

[74]

Carteret in 1679, claimed political jurisdiction over all New Jersey. Philip Carteret denied his right to interfere and warned him to keep his hands off. But, as we shall see, Andros was wanting in tact and harsh in carrying out his master's notions. Accordingly, he had Carteret arrested and tried for presuming to exercise authority within the Duke of York's patent. But the court upheld Carteret, and the duke himself finally reinstated him as governor.

The career of Andros in the New World was destined to be a memorable one, not only in regard to himself, but especially in regard to the colonists, due to the oppressive and arbitrary manner

THE LANDING OF CARTERET
From the Mural Decoration, Hudson County Court House, Jersey City, New Jersey

in which he carried out the orders of the masters whom he served. Though he was tyrannical in forcing his authority on New Jersey and the Long Island towns claiming to be under the jurisdiction of Governor Winthrop of Connecticut, he showed great efficiency in administering the affairs of the province of New York. The Duke of York was well satisfied with the way he served his interests there—so much so that he knighted his faithful deputy when in 1681 Andros returned to England to explain his official conduct in regard to his treatment of Philip Carteret, and also to justify himself as to many other complaints that had reached the ears of James. During the absence of Andros serious troubles

[75]

arose over customs duties which many of the New York merchants refused to pay, and to this revolt of the merchants there was added disaffection among the people, who made clamorous demands for a representative assembly. James had no sympathy for popular governments, believing that "nothing was more known than the aptness of such bodies to assume to themselves many privileges which prove destructive to or very oft disturb the peace of the government wherein they are allowed." But now, with the general disaffection of the people against the proprietary system of government and the falling off of the revenue receipts in his province of New York, James thought it wise to yield and to give New York a representative government like that enjoyed in the other colonies. In place of Andros, however, James now sent Thomas Dongan to be governor of New York, with instructions to issue writs for the election of a representative assembly, without whose consent the governor and his council could not levy taxes or make laws. Among the measures that the new assembly passed was the Charter of Franchises and Liberties, which was sent to James for his approval. Though he signed the charter, there was some delay in dispatching it to New York. In the interim Charles II died, February 6, 1685. The duke now became king and New York became a royal province to be administered henceforth by the Lords of

ENGLISH SOLDIER
From the Mural Decoration, Hudson County Court House, Jersey City, New Jersey

[76]

Trade. A new commission was sent to Governor Dongan, with no mention of a representative assembly, the powers of legislation and taxation once more to be vested in the governor and council alone. New York was to be annexed to the newly organized "dominion" of New England, and the same fate was to befall New Jersey and Delaware. It was the policy of James to annul the charters of all the colonies; to abolish all the independent governments and bring them under immediate dependence on the crown.

In 1684 the charter of Massachusetts had been overthrown. "The death of King Charles," says Wilson, "delayed a settlement; but James, when he came to the throne, very promptly showed what he meant to do. He resolved to put Massachusetts and the colonies lying immediately about her into the hands of a royal governor and an appointed council, without an assembly or any other arrangement of their affairs. At first (May, 1686) he named Joseph Dudley 'President of the Council for Massachusetts Bay, New Hampshire, and Maine, and the Narragansett country, or King's Province,' but gave him no authority to alter law or impose taxes. But that was only a temporary arrangement. The real change came with the arrival of Sir Edmund Andros, in December, 1686, to be 'Governor-General and Vice-Admiral'; and Plymouth was added to his government.

"Joseph Dudley had been unwelcome enough. It was a bitter thing for the people of Massachusetts to have this man, whom they deemed a traitor, nothing less, set over them. He was the son of Thomas Dudley, the stern Puritan of their day of first exile and settlement, who had been second to the great Winthrop in the founding of the colony. And now Thomas Dudley's son, once their agent in London to defend their charter,

From
Harper's Magazine, May, 1890
THE DRUMBEAT WOULD BE
HEARD IN THE CITY UPON THE
ARRIVAL OF A NEW GOVERNOR

[77]

had consented to serve the crown in the overthrow of their liberties. But Andros was worse. Dudley was at least timid and time-serving

From *Harper's Magazine*, June, 1883

GOVERNOR ANDROS AND THE BOSTON PEOPLE

and doubtful of his power; but Sir Edmund came with instructions and with a temper of command which no one could mistake. He

[78]

meant no rank injustice, indeed, but he was no statesman, knew only the rough way of the soldier in carrying out his instructions, and had very definite and unpalatable instructions to carry out. He was bidden appoint persons of the best character and estate to his council, and to disturb the existing law of the colonies as little as possible; but he was also commanded to allow no printing press within his jurisdiction; to insist upon a universal toleration in matters of religion—especially upon the encouragement of the worship of the Church of England; and to execute with vigilance and vigor the laws of trade. He was given, too, a small number of royal troops for his support, whose red coats were sadly unwelcome in Boston. Worst of all, he was authorized to govern and to lay taxes without an assembly.

"Happily, the new tyranny had no longer life in America than in England. It came promptly enough to its end when the news reached the colonies of James's disgrace and flight and William's coming" (to whom, with his wife Mary, daughter of James, Parliament had offered the crown in February, 1689). "The Boston people rose," continues Wilson, "as if by a common instinct; seized Andros and his officers; seized the fort; seized even the king's frigate lying in the harbor; and resumed their old government under their old magistrates, to await further tidings from over sea. The other colonies round about followed suit. Sir Edmund had got himself well hated. He was an honest, well-meaning man enough, a plain and not very quick-witted soldier who executed his orders quite literally; but he was arbitrary and harsh, and showed sometimes an unwise and ugly temper when he was opposed. And the orders he tried to execute were intolerable to the people of the once free colony he governed. He levied taxes by the authority of the crown; he demanded quitrents of all the land owners

[79]

of the colony, because the loss of the charter, he was told by the law officers in England, destroyed the right of the colonists to the land they had acquired under it; he forbade even the ordinary town meetings; and he sought to crush opposition by harsh punishments. To these Puritans it was no small part of the trying experience that he encouraged some to set up a society to worship after the manner of the Church of England, and use the hated Prayer-book; and that in 1688 the Episcopal congregation thus formed built a place of worship, which they called King's Chapel, in Boston. It was a happy day when they got rid of the hateful tyranny; and an assurance of better times when they presently learned that the new government at home approved what they had done, and were willing that they should send Sir Edmund and his fellow prisoners to England for trial.

SLOUGHTER SIGNS THE DEATH WARRANT OF LEISLER

"The action of the people was no less prompt and decisive in New York, James's own province. Francis Nicholson, Andros's deputy in New York and the Jerseys, was as little liked there as Andros himself was in Boston. Both he and the members of his council, because they supported him, were looked upon as tools of a papist king, and New York was Dutch and Protestant. The two regiments of the king's regulars Sir Edmund had brought with him upon his second coming out, to be governor of all the northern coast, were Irish Catholics every man, and Nicholson had come out as commander of one of them. To the uneasy suspicions of the critical Protestants of the little seaport affairs wore the ugly look of having brought them into the power of men who must of necessity prove the enemies of a Protestant king. With news of the revolution in England, moreover, came also news of war with France, the ousted king's Romish friend and ally; and the king's officers fell into an evident panic. While they hesitated what to do, a captain of the men at arms they had called together for their defense seized the fort and the government in the name of the Prince of Orange. This was Jacob Leisler. He had come to the colony close upon thirty years before (1660), as a soldier in the employ of the Dutch West India Company; had thriven in trade and made a place of influence for himself among the colonists; and now stepped forth as their champion against the officers of the papist king whom the Parliament had deposed. . . .

"As a matter of fact there was no danger. . . . But New York did not know how safe it was; and Leisler had his day. It might have been well enough had he stopped with thrusting Nicholson aside and assuming to play the new king's partisan and governor till the air should clear. But he did not. For a year and a half he maintained himself as governor, in the new

From *Harper's Magazine*, March, 1881
MYNHEER'S MORNING HORN

The decanter always filled with rum was a fixture in the Dutch home. Beside it stood a piece of a cow's horn smooth on each end and hollow. And every morning before breakfast Mynheer must "take a horn" as an appetizer.

[81]

king's name, but without his authority. He even resisted commissioned officers of the king until a governor sent from England came; and then he was hanged for treason.'' The new governor was Henry Sloughter, to whom some enemies of Leisler gave a banquet. Plying him with wine, he soon became intoxicated, and while in that state he was induced to sign the death warrant of this man who had been so loyal to his sovereigns. "It was a sad, unjust end. The man had been hot headed, arbitrary, blind, and willful, and had done much that the law could not sanction in order to have his own way; but he had done all, even that which was the

From *Harper's Magazine*, May, 1890

HOW THE ENGLISH IN NEW YORK
CELEBRATED THE ARRIVAL
OF A ROYAL GOVERNOR

deepest folly, in good faith. He had meant to serve the community he ruled, and had planned no treason against the king. There had been not a little of the heat of parties at the bottom of the trouble. The greater landowners, the king's officials, and the rich merchants had wished Nicholson to keep the government until the new king should send some one in his stead. The small tradesmen, the artisans, and the sailors of the town heard that there was war with France and that a French fleet was coming against the place,

Governor Sloughter Signing the Death Warrant
of Leisler

Illustration from
COLONIES AND NATION
by Woodrow Wilson

Originally published in
HARPER'S MAGAZINE, *April,* 1901

and believed that the rich men and the officials among them were no lovers of common men's liberties, or of a Protestant church, either; and Leisler was their leader. His condemnation was a thing resolved upon and hurried to its execution in New York, not commanded from oversea; and in 1695 Parliament itself took off the stain of treason from his name."

Though modifying the Stuart policy in many respects, William III found it wise to retain in his service the provincial officials who had served under Charles and James. Among them, Sir

From *Harper's Magazine*, May, 1896

OLD CAPITOL AT WILLIAMSBURG, VIRGINIA

Edmund Andros, whom we saw so hated at Boston, but against whom all charges were dismissed, still retained the royal confidence, for in 1691 he was, quoting again from Wilson's *History of the American People*, "once more commissioned governor, this time of Virginia, and stayed there full five years, a quieter if not a wiser man than in the days of King James. The Virginians did not wholly dislike him, taking him for what he was, a rough soldier,

An Interview Between Sir Edmund Andros and
James Blair

Illustration from
COLONIES AND NATION
by Woodrow Wilson

Originally published in
HARPER'S MAGAZINE, *April*, 1901

more efficient than patient, who meant to do his duty according to his instructions, but did not know how to do it in the wise way for his own interests and the general peace. He honestly devoted himself to the welfare of the colony, encouraged the growth of cotton in order that cloth might be made, improved the methods of administration, and sought in more than one way to better the sources of wealth. But the Virginians liked as little as the other colonists did his zeal in the enforcement of the acts of trade; and his arbitrary temper ruined him at last by bringing him into collision with James Blair.

"Andros's predecessor in the governorship of Virginia had been Francis Nicholson, a man who had been hardly more than a tool of James's tyranny a little while before in New York. . . . James Blair had found in him an intelligent friend, and not an opponent, when he sought to set up a college in the colony. A great deal of Virginian politics centered in Mr. Blair. He was a Scotsman bred to orders in the English Church, and was but thirty-six when Sir Edmund Andros was made governor of Virginia. He had come to the colony in 1685, at twenty-nine; and as the bishop's [Bishop of London] commissary there it was Mr. Blair's duty to inspect, report upon, and administer discipline in the church of the colony. He made it his first task to establish a college —the assembly, the governor, and every true friend of Virginia at his back in the enterprise—in order that education might sustain order and enlightenment. The king granted a charter and revenues to the college in 1692; the merchants of London subscribed right handsomely; Governor Nicholson handed over to it three hundred and fifty pounds voted to him by the assembly; and Virginia at last had the college she had wished and planned for ever since the days of Sir George Yeardley. It was agreed that it should be called the College of William and Mary.

"But when Sir Edmund Andros came, Mr. Nicholson being sent to administer the affairs of Maryland, it was found, after a few years' trial, that he and Mr. Blair could not live in the same colony. Mr. Blair was as hot tempered as Sir Edmund, and spoke his mind in as choleric and unstinted a way. But Mr. Blair, though he was often boisterous, generally managed, after the canny Scots manner, to be right as well, and generally had both the law and the interests of the colony on his side when it came to a contest, while Sir Edmund had a great talent for putting himself in the wrong. When at last it came to a breach between the two, therefore, as it did, Sir Edmund lost and Mr. Blair won. Sir Edmund was recalled to England, and Mr. Nicholson was named governor once more. It was a long time before Mr. Blair ceased to reign in Virginia. Mr. Nicholson became instrumental in removing the capital from Jamestown, which Mr. Bacon had burned, to Williamsburg, more wholesomely placed, ten miles back from the river. The college also had been placed there; and there Mr. Blair continued to preside as governors came and went."

From *Harper's Magazine*, November, 1882

Chapter V

HOW PENNSYLVANIA WAS FOUNDED

HEN Andros was governor of New York, it will be remembered he claimed that in granting East Jersey to Carteret the Duke of York had not conferred upon him any powers of government. The same condition Andros said also applied to West Jersey, which had fallen to the share of Lord Berkeley, to whom, jointly with Sir George Carteret, the entire province of New Jersey had been granted in 1664. In 1673 Lord Berkeley sold his share to two Quakers named John Fenwick and Edward Byllynge. Strangely enough for Quakers, the two partners quarreled over the division and the dispute was arbitrated by William Penn, who allotted nine-tenths of Berkeley's share to Byllynge, while the remaining tenth, with the payment of a sum of money, went to Fenwick. Later Byllynge was declared insolvent, and among the trustees for Byllynge's creditors was William Penn.

It was thus that Penn, as one of the Byllynge trustees, became

[88]

the owner of a share in the province of West Jersey, which was to result nine years later in the founding of Pennsylvania. This

From *Harper's Magazine*, November, 1882
"I OFTEN TOOK MY BIBLE AND SAT IN HOLLOW TREES"

was in 1673, when Penn was twenty-nine years old. He was born in 1644, the same year in which George Fox, the founder of the Society of Friends, or Quakers, then a young man of twenty, first began to preach his new doctrine. "He preached," says Wilson, "no new creed, but only simplicity and purity of life, the direct gift of a guiding light from heaven, without inter-mediation of priest or church or learned dogma, the independence of every man's conscience, and his freedom from the authority of man or government in such things as concerned the life of the spirit."

From Fox's journal of his own life we learn that as a boy he lived in solitude, suffering that travail of

[89]

spirit from which sprang the code of ethics which he afterward taught. Of this period he writes in his journal: "Sometimes kept myself retired in my chamber, and often walked solitary in the chase to wait upon the Lord. I wondered why these things should come to me. I looked upon myself and said, 'Was I ever so before?'" Again he says: "When it was day I wished for night, and when it was night I wished for day. . . . I fasted, walked much in solitary places many days, and often took my bible and sat in hollow trees and lonesome places till night came on. . . . But yet I had some intermissions from my troubles, and was sometimes brought into such a heavenly state that I thought I had been in Abraham's bosom."

And so when he was twenty he went forth into the world preaching repentance unto the people. He especially sought out fairs and market places where there would be revelry and merriment, and to the people there gathered he would remind them that life was short, calling upon them to repent and turn their eyes toward God. Describing one of such gatherings, he writes

From *Harper's Magazine*, November, 1882
"I SAT IN A HAYSTACK"

[90]

How Pennsylvania Was Founded

"I passed to another town where was another great meeting, the old priest (a late convert) being with me; and there came many professors (of religion) of several sorts to it. I sat in a haystack and said nothing for some hours, for I was to famish them from words. The professors kept asking the old priest when I would begin and when I would speak. He bade them wait, and told them that the people waited upon Christ a long time before he spoke. At last I was moved by the Lord to speak and they were struck by the Lord's power. The word of life reached them, and there was a general convincement amongst them."

Among the disciples of George Fox the most celebrated was William Penn, "so singularly unlike," says Wilson, "the plain, unlettered people who had been the first to hear Mr. Fox with gladness and live as he counseled." He was the son of Sir William Penn, admiral in the royal navy, the favorite of King Charles II, and the especial favorite of the Duke of York, who was later to become king. The old admiral had pinned his hopes on his son, for whom he expected a notable career; and when he turned Quaker and gave up everything for the principles of George Fox, the father was astounded and angered. There were many disagreements between them, "culminating at last when William, in spite of the earnest request of his father, refused to remove his hat even in the presence of the king and the Duke of York." Whereupon the admiral lost control of himself and in a rage ordered the son to quit the house. But when his first anger had cooled and he saw how dauntless his son held to his Quaker principles, young William was forgiven.

"And so it turned out," Wilson goes on to say, "that West Jersey was bought—so far as Mr. Penn and those who thought with him among the new proprietors were concerned—to be a refuge and place of peace for the Quakers. It was the Quakers who principally crowded into the new province and gave it its prosperity and its sober way in affairs. But Mr. Penn's plans widened as his thought became engaged in this great matter. A mere share in the ownership of West Jersey did not satisfy him. He determined to have a province of his own, a Quaker colony upon a great scale. The outcome of that purpose was the founding of Pennsylvania, whose peaceful story of orderly govern-

From *Harper's Magazine*, November, 1882

THE ADMIRAL LOST CONTROL OF HIMSELF

ment and quick prosperity reads like the incidents, almost, of an idyl amidst the confused annals of colonial affairs in that day of change. Sir William Penn had died in 1670, and had left to his son, among other items of an ample fortune, a claim for sixteen thousand pounds against the crown. The young Quaker asked for a grant of land in America in satisfaction of the claim, and the king readily enough consented, glad to please an old friend's son and be quit of an obligation so easily. Penn asked for and obtained the land 'lying north of Maryland, on the east bounded

Quaker and King at Whitehall

Illustration from
THE EARLY QUAKERS IN ENGLAND AND PENNSYLVANIA
by Howard Pyle

Originally published in
HARPER'S MAGAZINE, *November,* 1882

with Delaware River, on the west limited as Maryland is, and northward to extend as far as plantable' into the unclaimed Indian country; and the king pleased his own fancy by calling the grant "Pennsylvania," in honor of the old admiral whose claim against the crown he was thus paying off. The grant was dated March 4, 1681."

Although Penn acknowledged "that government was a business he had never undertaken," he determined that the colonists already settled in his province should be "at the mercy of no governor," but that they should "live a free, and" he hoped, "a sober and industrious people." His new province was to be a place of refuge for the sect whom so many at home despised and persecuted, while he himself would put his faith and all his fortune in this "holy experiment" he was to make in the New World. It was Penn's belief "that any government is free to the people under it (whatever be the frame) where the laws rule and the people are a party to those laws."

From the time when Penn received his grant from Charles II in 1681, immigrants began flocking to his province, making settlements along the western shore of the Delaware River from the Schuylkill to New Castle. "In August, 1682," remarks Wilson, "Mr. Penn added to his first grant from the king the lands lying about New Castle and below by purchase from the Duke of York." By this addition the province gained an outlet to the sea, which Mr. Penn was determined to have, in spite of the protests of Maryland.

In August, 1682, Penn with a company of colonists, most of whom were Quakers, sailed for the New World in the good ship *Welcome*. Of the one hundred emigrants who embarked at Deal thirty died of smallpox during the voyage of two months. At length the *Welcome* rounded the Capes of Delaware Bay, and three days later, October 27th, the storm-beaten ship dropped her anchor in front of the town of New Castle. There she was boarded by commissioners representing Sir Edmund Andros,

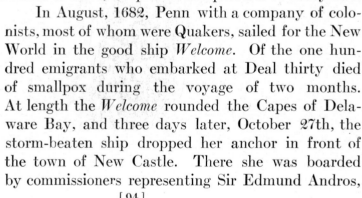

William Penn in Conference with the Colonists

Illustration from
THE FIRST VISIT OF WILLIAM PENN TO AMERICA
Originally published in
HARPER'S WEEKLY, *March 31*, 1883

governor of New York, who examined his deeds of enfeoffment granted him by the Duke of York. Finding these to be correct, the commissioners surrendered to Mr. Penn the fort of New Castle "by giving him the key thereof to lock upon himself alone the door, which being opened again by him, we did deliver also unto him one turf with a twig upon it . . . in part of all what was specified in the said deed of enfeoffment from his royal highness."

FIRST VISIT OF WILLIAM PENN TO AMERICA

Upon his landing at New Castle an enthusiastic reception was given him by the settlers who had

From *Harper's Magazine*, November, 1882

DEPARTURE OF THE "WELCOME"

A Pennsylvania Cave-Dwelling, XVIIth Century

Illustration from
COLONIES AND NATION
by Woodrow Wilson

Originally published in
HARPER'S MAGAZINE, *April,* 1901

already founded a flourishing settlement there. Not only Friends, but members of other denominations—Englishmen, Swedes, and Germans—joined in giving him a cordial welcome. Several conferences were held, a charter of liberties was issued, a democratic form of government was instituted, and the city of Philadelphia was planned and founded. At this time also was made the cele-

From *Harper's Magazine*, November, 1882

WILLIAM PENN AND THE COMMISSIONERS IN THE CABIN OF THE "WELCOME"

brated treaty with several Indian tribes—the only treaty, says Voltaire, "never sworn to and never broken."

"The chief town of the province," in the words of Wilson, "was established at the confluence of the two fine rivers Delaware and Schuylkill, and Mr. Penn named it Philadelphia, wishing it to be a place of peace and good will. At first those who were to build there lived in caves cut out of the bluffs which lined the river; but they were quick at substituting good houses. By the end of the year 1683 there were no fewer than one hundred and fifty dwellings built—frail and cheap enough, no doubt, but sufficient until stone and brick could be had, and time in which to build with them. The change came very soon. The sober, substantial, yeomanlike folk who came into the colony preferred, whenever it was possible, to build of good, lasting stuff, and to build solidly and well. Before Mr. Penn sailed for home, in 1684, there were already three hundred and fifty houses erected, some of them several stories high, built with cellars and decorated with balconies. Outside the central town, with its busy two thousand colonists, there were quite fifty hamlets in the thriving province."

Where Penn found a measureless wilderness of forest, we behold a country teeming with population, ripe in wealth, and strong in the beneficent government which he founded. William Penn was destined never to establish himself in this country as he desired to do; twice he attempted it, but in both cases, after a short stay, he returned again to England. His province never brought him anything but trouble and perplexity. But such a government as he established, and such a land as he planted, are in themselves sufficient compensation for the best endeavor of any man's life. They will carry his name down through many years of time, in the emptiness of which it would long since have been forgotten but for this his ripest life's work.

Chapter VI

SALEM, MASSACHUSETTS, IN 1692

T will be remembered that, following the overthrow in 1688 of Sir Edmund Andros, the first royal governor of New England, the people of Massachusetts set up a provisional government under which they governed themselves for nearly three years entirely independent of the king of England. In 1691 a new charter was granted by King William III which Sir William Phips, the newly appointed governor of Massachusetts, brought with him in the spring of 1692.

PHIPS RECOVERS THE SUNKEN TREASURE

Wilson records: "It was something to have one of their own fellow colonists, a familiar figure among them, at least, for their first governor under the new arrangement, though that did not alter his powers, and he was hardly the man they would themselves have chosen. Sir William Phips was only a rough, pushing, self-made sailor, one of the youngest of the twenty-one sons of a humble gunsmith in a little settlement close by the mouth of the far-away Kennebec. He had been a ship's carpenter, a common seaman,

Phips Recovering the Sunken Treasure

Illustration from
COLONIES AND NATION
by Woodrow Wilson

Originally published in
HARPER'S MAGAZINE, *April,* 1901

a ship's captain—always sanguine, always adventurous, always on the make, risking everything to win his way, and as cheerful and hearty and full of confident plans when he had lost as when he had won. At last he had actually made the fortune he was in quest of, by finding and recovering the treasure of a sunken Spanish galleon in the southern seas. He had been much in England, and had won favor in the court and out of it by his bluff and honest energy and unfailing good will, and his breezy manners brought fresh from the salt seas. King James had knighted him Sir William for the Spanish treasure he brought into England, and had made him high sheriff of New England when Sir Edmund Andros was governor there. In the year 1690, the year before the new charter was signed, he had led an expedition into the north and taken Acadia from the French, with much excellent private plunder, and then had failed in an expedition against Quebec. He was no statesman, and it was not pleasant for any man to be the first governor under the new charter; but bluff Sir William, known to every man in Boston, was better than a stranger might have been."

In the very first year of Sir William's governorship a terrible distemper broke out at Salem village—a distemper of the mind which spread like a plague until its contagion had affected the minds of all the people with a deadly fear—the fear that is ever present when terror reigns. This madness, this frenzy which seized upon the people of Salem in the year 1692, produced that great tragedy of New England history known as the Witchcraft Delusion.

So many persons had been accused of witchcraft during the winter of 1692, that when the new governor arrived in May of that year he found the jails in Boston and vicinity overflowing with persons awaiting trial. To alleviate the crowded condition of the jails, as well as to grant the accused the right of immediate trial, to which they were entitled, he at once appointed a special term of the superior court to hear the cases. But the dread superstition held as great sway over the minds of the court as it had over the minds of the multitude. During the period of its sweep—and

Arresting a Witch

Illustration from
THE SECOND GENERATION OF ENGLISHMEN IN AMERICA
by Thomas Wentworth Higginson
Originally published in
HARPER'S MAGAZINE, *July,* 1883

the evil lasted one long year—nineteen persons, the majority of them women, were convicted and rode to the gallows in the hangman's cart.

What was this witchcraft which took as great a hold upon the intelligent men and women of Salem as it did upon the unlearned, superstitious populace? A witch was a person, usually an old woman, supposed to have made a compact with the devil. Becoming the devil's agent, it became her mission to conspire against good people, casting evil spells upon them and often causing the death of those against whom she held spite or envy.

All witches had an appointed place of meeting. Obedient to the call of his satanic majesty, in whose book they had signed their names in blood, the apparitions of these bewitched persons— toothless old hags in short petticoats, white linen hoods, and conical high-crowned hats, came flocking in the dead of night, on flying broomsticks, to the witches' trysting place.

The trysting place of the Salem witches was supposed to have been in the pasture of the Rev. Samuel Parris, pastor of the church in Salem village. It was at his house that the witchcraft delusion of 1692 had its rise. During the winter of 1691–92 eight young girls, among them the minister's daughter and his niece, used to meet in the minister's kitchen, where they practiced some of the now well-known tricks of magic, which they learned from the minister's Indian servant. Soon the strange actions of these girls attracted the notice of Mr. Parris. Neither the girls themselves nor their elders could explain their actions. They grew very strange and wild when they were asked what ailed them. They would immediately scream out, or fall to weeping, utter foolish talk, and sometimes fly into a furious rage, as though seized with a frenzy. Doctors were called in, but these learned men were mystified at the "disease" which they declared was unknown to medical science. Some explanation of the ailment, however, was necessary, and when the doctors agreed that the girls had been bewitched— possessed of the devil—great alarm arose in the whole community. Private and public fasts were held not only in the immediate

[104]

"Hey, Black Cat! Hey, My Pretty Black Cat"

*Desiring to afflict her mistress for an imaginary slight, the old
woman goes to the fireplace, looks up the chimney, and cries:
"Hey, black cat! my pretty black cat! Go ye and sit on my
mistress's breast, and claw her if she stirs. Do as I bid ye, my
pretty black cat, and I'll sign the book."*

Illustration from
GILES COREY, YEOMAN
by Mary E. Wilkins

Originally published in
HARPER'S MAGAZINE, *December,* 1892

vicinity, but in other parts of Massachusetts. At first the girls refused to tell anything about the cause of their troubles, but at length, fearing punishment from their parents and not realizing the consequences of their accusation, they named three old women by whom they claimed to have been bewitched.

THE WITCHCRAFT FRENZY

Afterward similar charges were made against other persons, until finally the jails of Boston and Salem were filled with the victims of this mad frenzy, and before the year was out the denunciations of these eight simple country girls were to cost the lives of nineteen persons for an imaginary crime. Perhaps a mere spirit of mischief at first caused the girls to make these false accusations, and when they saw the result of their falsehood, fear for what might happen to themselves led them farther. Perhaps the girls really believed in their own powers of magic; no wonder if they did, for the universal belief of the time in witchcraft and the excited state of the people, due to fear of war with the French and their savage allies, rendered a ready belief by the people in their charges, supported as they were by the judges themselves. Maybe in calmer times intelligence would have ruled and prevented that harvest of death which justifies our calling the year 1692 the dark age of New England history.

Many were the signs and portents of that tragic year when witches were so malignant at Salem. The skeptical, as well as the ignorant and credulous, had fear in their hearts. Nobody cared to travel far at night; not even the bravest would enter a churchyard. It was most dangerous to be a crabbed old woman; terror held all such in its grasp, as mere suspicion or the prejudice of their neighbors might bring them to the gallows.

THE SALEM WOLF [1]

All sorts of stories were told and believed. Among them was one about Granny Good, a crabbed, melancholy old woman of ill repute, one of the three women accused by the girls as having

[1] Adapted from a story by Howard Pyle, *Harper's Magazine*, December, 1909.

Giles Corey in Prison

Among the last to suffer death for the imaginary crime of
witchcraft at Salem in 1692 was old Giles Corey, who, refusing to
answer any questions on his trial, was pressed to death. This is
the only known instance in America of the infliction of this
penalty, called in French, peine forte et dure, *or pressing to death.*

Illustration from
GILES COREY, YEOMAN
by Mary E. Wilkins

Originally published in
HARPER'S MAGAZINE, *December, 1892*

bewitched them. The thing happened in October of the year preceding her ride to Gallows Hill. The poor old woman was destitute and, happening by a neighbor's house, she asked to come in, and was refused. Whereupon, as was said, she went off muttering. The hired man was for giving her something, fearing she might

From *Harper's Magazine*, December, 1892

A SALEM MAID OF 1692 SPINNING FLAX OR, AS IT WAS CALLED
"DOING HER STINT," HER LOVER LOOKING ON WITHAL

cast the evil eye on the family; and sure enough, when he went out to look after her, there she was at the corner of the road, scowling at the house. "She spat upon the ground," so said the hired man, "and shook her fist at him, all skin and bone, and withered like a dead leaf." Then she cried: "Your master will be sorry for this; for I curse him once!—I curse him twice!—I curse him thrice!" Then she went away down the road, leaving the hired man all atremble with fear.

A Wolf Had Not Been Seen at Salem
for Thirty Years

Illustration from
THE SALEM WOLF
by Howard Pyle

Originally published in
HARPER's MAGAZINE, *December,* 1909

The Trial of a Witch

The accusing girls are pointing at their victim and crying out,
" There is a flock of yellow birds around her head."

Illustration from
GILES COREY, YEOMAN
by Mary E. Wilkins

Originally published in
HARPER'S MAGAZINE, *December*, 1892

The very next day the master's best cow died. "That is the first curse come true," said the hired man. A week later he found his master's best ox unable to rise from the ground where he had left him to rest, and however hard he tried to raise him to the yoke, he couldn't, and the ox was never good for anything afterward. "This is the second curse come true," said the hired man. Not long following these two visitations of witchcraft, as those believed who heard the story, the master's daughter Miriam began to act strangely. She would not rise out of bed for days at a time, and would mutter all sorts of strange and wild things. Her lover was sure that she was bewitched, but for a long time Miriam would say nothing. Finally she confessed that Granny Good had bewitched her. Her story was like that of the girls at the minister's house.

One day, while Miriam was turning the bread in the oven, the kitchen door opened and a great black cat came running in. Though she raised the bread peel to strike at the cat, it only ran round and round the room and would not leave. Suddenly the cat was gone and in its place stood Granny Good looking at her. The girl could not move a single

"Dark, dim, Dante-like solitudes."

From "The Broomstick Train" by Oliver Wendell Holmes, Houghton, Mifflin & Company, 1892 hair, so terrified was she. Then the old woman "plucked three hairs out of her own head and came to where Miriam sat; and she tied the three hairs about the girl's finger." It seems that that magic performance made Miriam a witch from that time on, for she even went once or twice to the devil's meeting house.

Such was the story that Miriam told. Sure enough, they found a ring of hair tied about her little finger. Her mother cut the hairs with a pair of scissors and left her. The family now felt happy, believing that the removal of the hair ring would restore Miriam to her normal self.

But Miriam was better only a very short time, and within a few days she was as wild as ever. Shortly after Granny Good was tried for witchcraft. Miriam's father was present at Gallows Hill, and when the old woman saw him she cried out: "Ah! You have come to see me hanged, have you! Well, then, look to yourself; the third curse is still upon you, and something worse than hanging will happen to you before the year is out."

Now that the old witch was hanged, everyone thought that Miriam would be cured of the spell that had been cast upon her. But it was not so. She became worse than ever, and ran away so often at night that a watch was set upon her. She managed, however, to avoid all vigilance, and when she would return in the early dawn she acted like a wild, starving creature

[111]

Early in the winter of that year a wolf appeared in Salem. "Such a thing as a wolf had not been seen at Salem for thirty years and more, and folks were slow to believe that it really was a wolf that killed the sheep . . . that every now and then were found dead and part eaten in the morning.

"But afterward everybody knew it was a wolf; for one night Eli Hackett saw it as he was coming home from town meeting. . . . After that several others saw the wolf at different times, and once

it chased Doctor Wilkinson on a dark night for above a half mile and into the very town itself. Then so many people saw the wolf that women and children were afraid to go out after nightfall, and even men would not go out without an ax or club."

One night the wolf was seen in the yard of Miriam's father. Its howls awoke the hired man, who took a shot at it from the attic window. The noise of the firing awoke the whole house. All the family came into the kitchen, except Miriam. The hired man was sure his aim had not missed the beast, for the moonlight made everything as light as day. As they stood about discussing the affair, Miriam suddenly came in as still as a ghost, clad only in her shift and petticoat. She did not appear to see those standing about, but went straight off to her room. Her mother began to cry. Seeing that her daughter walked thus in her sleep, she feared the wolf would kill her some night as it prowled about.

Once It Chased Doctor Wilkinson into the
Very Town Itself

Illustration from
THE SALEM WOLF
by Howard Pyle

Originally published in
HARPER'S MAGAZINE, *December,* 1909

For a while after this the wolf did not appear, and people said the musket-shot had scared it away. But it came back again in a few days. This time several persons saw it, and more cattle were found dead in the morning than before. But worst of all, a man was found dead one morning in his back yard, his neck so torn and rent that only the wolf could have done it.

Meanwhile, everybody was wondering what ailed Miriam, and most of all her sweetheart was anxious to know. Such things were being said about her that he must know whether they were true; otherwise he could not marry her. The mother went to fetch Miriam from her room. Although night had long since fallen, the girl was nowhere to be seen, and her mother knew she was sleep walking again. Miriam's father was not at home, having gone to town with a load of potatoes. But he would soon return, and perhaps he could explain away all these stories about his daughter.

Just then the good man's sledge appeared in the road, but as the horse came running through the gate the sledge was seen to be empty, with Miriam's father nowhere in sight. Nothing but the dreadful wolf could have caused this, and without delay Miriam's sweetheart, with the hired man, jumped into the sledge and drove away in a fury. They had not gone very far "when, all of a sudden, the horse stopped stock-still with a jerk that nearly threw them both out of the sledge." Upon their standing up in the sledge they saw the wolf attacking Miriam's father, who lay in the snow like one dead. While the hired man held the leaping and plunging horse, Miriam's sweetheart, armed with an ax, rushed upon the wolf, and with one yell he struck the beast upon the neck with his ax just where the neck joins the shoulder. "With that the wolf instantly let go the man and whirled about several times in the road, howling and yelling." As it ran, shaking its head, blood was sprinkled upon the snow all the way until it disappeared in the woods. Miriam's father, however, was only in a swoon, and came to soon after he was placed in the sledge. He was badly cut and torn about the neck and shoulder, and but for the heavy collar of his fur coat the wolf might have killed him.

Lights were moving within the house as they approached, and when they entered, Miriam's mother cried out that Miriam had just returned, sorely hurt. When they went to her room they found Miriam in bed, "with a sheet drawn up to her chin, and the sheet was all stained red with blood. Upon pulling the sheet down over her shoulders a great, terrible deep wound was seen in the girl's neck where the neck joins the shoulder, and the bed beneath her was all soaked with blood."

As to how she got her injury at first the girl would not tell, only "whimpering and whining just as a great dog would do." But when her lover bade her, in the name of God, to tell him how she came by her hurt, she cried out: "Torture me not and I will tell you all! I walked in my sleep. I walked out into the barn, and I walked on the haymow, and all the while I was asleep. I slipped from the haymow and I fell on the scythe and cut my neck." And sure enough, when they went the next day to look, they found blood in the barn where the scythe hung. But they also saw that the blood was in the very spot where she had stood while putting on her shift and petticoat before she went into the house. As for the girl herself, her wound festered and she died of fever a few days later.

Many stories such as the above were told that year in Salem village. However marvelous these tales might be, ready credit was given to the wildest fancying of minds disordered by the happenings of that terrible year.

Part *II*
The French Come Upon the Scene

Chapter I

FIRST FRENCH EFFORTS TO PLANT COLONIES IN THE NEW WORLD

OR France as well as for England, America was the land of opportunity—a wilderness empire beyond the seas. Somewhere along its shores was to be found the long-sought river flowing into the western ocean that would lead to Cathay and the wealth of the Indies. It was natural for Francis I, King of France, to look with longing eyes toward this land of mystery whose wealth he saw flowing these many years into the treasury of his hated rival, Charles V, who laid claim to all this vast territory by virtue of the discoveries of Columbus. England also claimed these lands as her right by reason of the discoveries of the two Cabots. But now it was time for France to make her claim to a share in this rich prize, basing her rights on the voyage which Verazzano had made to the shores of America in 1524.

The rivalry of France, however, for the possession of this hemisphere of the New World was not to be with Spain, now already decaying, but with England, whose sons, like her own, were full of the life and vigor of youth and primed for the great enterprise, in which the stake was to be the winning or losing of a continent.

JACQUES CARTIER SETS UP A CROSS AT GASPÉ

In 1534 Philippe de Brion-Chabot, the boon companion of Francis I, was also Admiral of France. He was quick to realize that the way to make good the claims of his country to the lands in the New World discovered by Verazzano was to take actual possession. Chabot knew just the man for this purpose—Jacques Cartier, a master pilot of St.-Malo, who had sailed from that nursery of the sailors of France for years on fishing voyages to the coast of Labrador. No better man could have been chosen as the agent to build up a new France beyond the sea. Accordingly, April 20, 1534, Cartier sailed from St.-Malo, under the commands of his royal master, to steer his course with the definite purpose of formally extending the bounds of France. Reaching Newfoundland without mishap, he sailed into the Bay of Chaleurs and set up a cross at Gaspé—a peninsula projecting from the mainland of Canada— telling the natives there with pious fraud that it was only intended for a beacon.

"After touching at Newfoundland," writes R. G. Thwaites in his *France in America*, "he explored the St. Lawrence until land could be seen on either side. The next year he repeated his voyage, and, ascending to Lachine Rapids, the head of navigation from the sea, named the island mountain at their foot Mont-Royal. His report of a winter's experience (1535–36) in this inhospitable climate, near the gray cliff of Quebec, gave pause to Frenchmen in their western colonizing schemes; further, the king was now engaged at home in serious difficulties with Spain, and had neither thought, time, nor money for continuing the exploration of North America.

"When at last a truce had been declared between France and Spain, Cartier was made captain general and pilot of a new fleet of five vessels which was to bear to America the king's viceroy, Jean François de la Roche, better known as Roberval, from his estates in Picardy. A month later than the time set, Roberval having failed to arrive, Cartier set sail with three ships (May, 1541) and in August was again at Quebec, where he built a post

Jacques Cartier Setting Up a Cross at Gaspé

Illustration from
THE FRENCH VOYAGEURS
by Thomas Wentworth Higginson

Originally published in
HARPER'S MAGAZINE, *March,* 1883

which he abandoned in the spring, thence returning to France. It is said that in the Gulf of St. Lawrence he met the belated Roberval coming with supplies and with colonists who had for this purpose been liberated from French jails. The Picard remained for a year at Quebec, whose crude fortifications he restored and bettered, and he attempted some interior exploration. There are reports that Cartier was sent to bring him home in 1543. After the king's settlement of the accounts of the joint expedition (April 3, 1544) both Cartier and Roberval pass from our view."

Higginson in his *History of the United States* says: "For the first French efforts at actual colonization we must look southward on the map of America again, and trace the career of a different class of Frenchmen. After Villegagnon and his Huguenots had vainly attempted a colony at Rio Janeiro in 1555, Jean Ribaut, with other Huguenots, made an actual settlement seven years later, upon what is now the South Carolina coast, sailing to what is now the St. John's River, and, arriving on May Day, they called it 'River of the May.' Here they were received by a picturesque crowd of savages, wading into the water up to their shoulders and bringing little baskets of maize and of white and red mulberries, while others offered to help their visitors ashore. Sailing farther north, they entered Port Royal Harbor. Here they left behind a colony of thirty men. The lonely colonists spent a winter of absolute poverty and wretchedness. They built for themselves vessels in which they sailed for France, reaching it after sufferings too great to tell.

"Still another French Protestant colony followed in 1564, led by René de Laudonnière. He, too, sought the 'River of the May,' and built above what is now called St. John's Bluff, on the river of that name, a stronghold called Fort Caroline.

"The career of the colony was a tragedy. Fort Caroline was built; the colonists mutinied and sought to become buccaneers, calling those who would not join them 'cowards and greenhorns.' Failing miserably in this, and wearing out the patience of their generous Indian friends, they almost perished of famine. There were plenty of adventurers, but no agriculturists. The English

Hawkins visited and relieved them. Ribaut came from France and again gave them aid, and their lives were prolonged only to meet cruel destruction from the energy and perfidy of a Spaniard, Don Pedro de Menendez. He came with a great squadron of thirty-four vessels—his flagship being nearly a thousand tons burden—to conquer and settle the vast continent then known as Florida. Menendez overcame the little colony, and then, after giving a pledge,

From *Harper's Magazine*, March, 1883

HE BROUGHT BOTH CATHOLIC PRIESTS AND HUGUENOT MINISTERS

written and sealed, to spare their lives, he proceeded to massacre every man in cold blood, sparing only a drummer, a fifer, and a fiddler. It is the French tradition that he hanged his prisoners on trees, with this inscription: 'I do this not as to Frenchmen, but as to Lutherans.' This was the same Menendez who in that same year (1565) had founded the Spanish colony of St. Augustine, employing for this purpose the negro slaves he had brought from Africa—the first introduction, probably, of slave labor upon the soil now included in the United States.

"The act of Menendez aroused a terrible demand for vengeance

[123]

in France, and this eager desire was satisfied by a Frenchman—this time by one who was probably not a Huguenot, but a Catholic. Dominique de Gourgues had been chained to the oar as a galley slave when a prisoner to the Spaniards, and, finding his king unable or unwilling to avenge the insult given to his nation in America, De Gourgues sold his patrimony that he might organize an expedition of his own. It is enough to say that he absolutely annihilated, in 1568, the colony that Menendez had left behind him in Florida, and hanged the Spaniards to the same trees where they had hanged

From *Harper's Magazine*, March, 1883
DOMINIQUE DE GOURGUES AVENGING THE MURDER OF THE HUGUENOT COLONY

the French, nailing above them this inscription: 'I do this not as to Spaniards or Moors (Marannes), but as to traitors, robbers, and murderers.'

"All these southern and Protestant colonies failed at last. It was farther north, in the lands of the most zealous of Roman Catholics, and in the regions explored long since by Cartier, that the brilliant career of French colonization in America was to have its course. Out of these voyages had grown temporary settlements, and the fur trade sprang up by degrees at Anticosti, at Sable Island, and especially at Tadousac. Through this trade Frenchmen learned the charm of the wilderness, and these charms attracted then, as always, a very questionable class of men. Cartier, in 1541, was authorized to ransack the prisons for malefactors. De la Roche, in 1598, brought a crew of convicts. De Monts, in 1604, was authorized to impress idlers and vagabonds for his colony. To keep them in order he brought both Catholic priests and Huguenot ministers, who disputed heartily on the way. 'I have seen our curé and the minister,' said Champlain, in Parkman's translation, 'fall to with their fists on questions of faith. I cannot say which had the more pluck, or which hit the harder, but I know that the minister sometimes complained to the Sieur de Monts that he had been beaten.'"

Among the colonists who came with De Monts in 1604 to the Bay of Fundy, was Samuel de Champlain, who established the first permanent French settlement at Quebec, in 1608, and discovered Lake Champlain and Lake Huron. He was not only a great explorer, but a good artist and a graceful writer, and in his journals has recorded all that he saw and heard in the course of his travels. In them we find minute descriptions of the Indians with whom he held relations similar to those of other Frenchmen—for the most part kindly and generous. "His most formidable act of kindness, if such it may be called," Higginson writes, "was when he first revealed to them the terrible power of firearms. He it was, of all men, who began for them that series of lessons in the military art by which the Frenchmen doubled the terrors of Indian warfare" and formed "that alliance which in later years made the phrase 'French and Indian' the symbol of all that was most to be dreaded in the way of conflict. He describes picturesquely an occasion when he and his Algonquin allies marched together against the Iroquois; and his Indians told him if he could only kill three particular chiefs for them they should win the day." When the Iroquois approached with the three chiefs in front wearing plumes, "Champlain told his allies that he was very sorry they could not understand his language better, for he could teach them such order and method in attacking their enemies that they would be sure of victory, but meanwhile he would do what he could. Then they called upon him with loud cries to stand forward, and so, putting him twenty paces in front, they advanced. Halting within thirty paces of the enemy, he rested

9 [125]

HE RESTED HIS MUSKET

his musket against his cheek and aimed at one of the chiefs. Two chiefs fell dead, and another man was mortally wounded. The effect upon the Iroquois must have been like that of fire from heaven. These chiefs were dressed in armor made of cotton fiber, and arrow-proof, yet they died in an instant. The courage of the whole band gave way, and when another Frenchman fired a shot from the woods they all turned and fled precipitately, abandoning camp and provisions—a whole tribe, and that one of the bravest, routed by the shots from French muskets."

This was in July, 1609. In the Indian wars that were to follow, the French, who had won the hearts of the Indians, were able to control the interior of the continent. But what was to save the English colonies was the fact that the French influence was not quite universal. Although white men had forgotten the attack made by Champlain and a few Frenchmen on an Iroquois fort, the Iroquois, otherwise known as the Five Nations, never forgot nor forgave. "They were always and ever ready, after that fatal day," writes Wilson in his *History of the American People*, "to be any man's ally, whether Dutch or English, against the hated French." This hostility, as it happened, proved to be the factor that lost to the French the North American continent. "For now," continues Wilson, "the French found it necessary to keep at the back of the broad forests which stretched from the eastern lakes to the Hudson and the Delaware, the wide empire of these dusky foes, astute, implacable."

Chapter II

THE DREAM OF LA SALLE

FOLLOWING the death of Champlain, the father of New France, who died in 1635 at Quebec, the city he had founded, the influence of the Jesuits became supreme in the colony. Their main object, of course, was the conversion of the Indians, which, combined with their interest in the fur trade, soon took them as far west as the outlet of Lake Superior, and, but for the outbreak of war between the Iroquois and the Hurons in 1649, might well have brought them to the Mississippi itself. But the attainment of this goal was destined to be the work of others—first, Father Marquette and Joliet, who floated down the Father of Waters for hundreds of miles in the year 1673, to be followed in 1682 by René Robert Cavelier, Sieur de la Salle, who accomplished his heart's desire by descending the river to its mouth.

In 1664 affairs took on a different look in this wilderness empire, by the arrival of new leaders sent out by Louis XIV, accompanied by a great influx of fresh colonists as well as a veteran body of twelve hundred infantry, whose main object was to put an end to the incursions of the terrible Iroquois whose raids to the northward so greatly endangered the northwestern fur trade, the development of which, together with the conversion of the heathens, was the main objects of the French.

Many of the settlers of the New World had not been selected for their sterling qualities, and as the population increased and but meager returns were to be gained from tilling the soil, these people, many of whom belonged to the lesser nobility, took more and more to a life of adventure and the pursuit of the fur trade. Frequently they were unable to secure a government license, but as so many of them were "ne'er-do-wells" and unwilling to do steady work, they became *coureurs de bois*, or illegal traders. Those practicing this calling rendered themselves subject to the penalty of outlawry, but in most cases the extreme punishment was seldom meted out. Becoming renegades of civilization, these men, to quote Thwaite, "readily fraternized with the savages, whose dress and manners they often affected, and, seldom possessing refined sentiments, frequently led Indian war parties in bloody forays upon the frontiers of the detested English—disguised by grease paint, breech clout, and feathers, and outdoing their followers in cruelty." And as we learn from Charlevoix, these *coureurs de bois*, having little will to civilize their savage companions, were themselves barbarized by the contact.

It was in the year 1666 that René Robert Cavelier, Sieur de la Salle, arrived in Canada from his native Rouen, where he had been born in the year 1643. His elder brother, Jean Cavelier, a priest of St.-Sulpice, was in Canada before him, and perhaps this circumstance had some influence upon his coming. At any rate, he found in Canada an ample field for his adventurous nature, and although he became the seigneur of La Chine, by accepting the feudal grant of a tract of land from the Sulpitians of Montreal he never again gave up the main purpose of his coming to America, which was to explore the wilderness and to find a route to China. By reason of his being possessed of this thought it is said that he named his estate La Chine, because he believed it was situated on the route to China.

During these first years in Canada he spent much time among the Indians, and heard from the Senecas of a great river which rose in their country, and on which, after a voyage of many months, it would be possible to reach the ocean by way of the northern lakes. La Salle concluded that this great river led into the Gulf of California or, as he called it, the "Vermilion Sea," and that by reaching

Coureurs de Bois

Illustration from
CANADIAN VOYAGEURS ON THE SAGUENAY
by C. H. Farnham
Originally published in
HARPER'S MAGAZINE, *March, 1888*

it he would gain the goal which all explorers in the Mississippi Valley up to this time had sought in vain. In his endeavors to come upon this river, it is claimed that in 1671 he reached the Falls of the Ohio (Louisville), which, in fact, was the river meant by the Senecas, and also that about this same date, prior to the expedition of Father Marquette, he had actually reached the Mississippi. But there is not sufficient evidence to substantiate this claim, and there are good grounds for disbelieving it.

LA SALLE PETITIONS THE KING FOR PERMISSION TO EXPLORE THE MISSISSIPPI

In 1673, however, we find him commandant of Fort Frontenac, which had been erected by Frontenac, the governor of the province, and in the following year, having learned of the achievement of Joliet and Father Marquette, he resolved to complete the work they had begun by himself tracing the unknown river to its mouth and setting up the standard of France, thereby gaining for his king the sovereignty over all the country from the Northern Ocean to the Gulf of Mexico. Frontenac strongly supported La Salle in his petitions to King Louis XIV, and at length, in May, 1678, a patent was granted him to explore the Mississippi to its mouth. After obtaining all the money he could borrow or secure in France, everything was made ready for the grand enterprise which was to result in his being the first white man to descend the Mississippi to its mouth, and the satisfaction of accomplishing his long-cherished vision of empire which gave to France the whole Mississippi Valley.

"On the 14th of July, 1678," to quote from the narrative of Charlevoix in his *Histoire de la Nouvelle France*, "la Sale and Tonti embarked at Rochelle with thirty men, including pilots and mechanics, and they reached Quebec on the 15th of September. Their stay there was short, because they wished to profit by the pleasant season to proceed to Catarocouy, whither they took with them Father Louis Hennepin, a Flemish Recollect, who subsequently accompanied them in most of their journeys. La Sale's

La Salle Petitions the King for Permission
to Explore the Mississippi

Illustration from
THE GREAT LA SALLE
by Henry Loomis Nelson

Originally published in
HARPER'S MAGAZINE, *February,* 1905

first care on arriving at Catarocouy was to begin his labors on the fort, which was only of palisades; he at the same time built a bark, and these operations were carried through with a celerity which gave a high idea of the activity of the new governor.

"He then sailed in his bark as far as Niagara, where he traced a new fort: this he confided to the Chevalier de Tonti, to whom he left thirty men, gave orders for building a second bark at the head of Lake Erie, above Niagara Falls, traversed on foot all the Seneca canton, made during the rest of the winter a number of other excursions, which had no other object than the fur trade, returned by land to Catarocouy, and sent his bark back to Niagara, loaded with provisions and merchandise.

"About the middle of August, the bark which had been built at the entrance of Lake Erie, being in a state to sail, la Sale embarked with forty men, including three Recollect Fathers, and steered for Michillimakinac.

"From Michillimakinac, the *Griffin* (so his bark was called) sailed to the Bay (Green Bay), from which point de la Sale sent it back to Niagara, loaded with furs. For his own part, he proceeded in a canoe to St. Joseph's River, where there was then a Miami town, at which Father Allouez was laboring with considerable success. Here the Chevalier de Tonti proceeded to join him. They did not remain there long. Tonti descended to the Illinois, and la Sale returned to Catarocouy, where he learned, on his arrival, that little doubt was entertained of the loss of the *Griffin*. In fact, no very authentic tidings were heard of it after it left the Bay.

"La Sale took a number of young Illinois, whom he found well disposed, and began to prepare in earnest to begin his explorations. He first detached a man named Dacan with Father Hennepin to ascend the Misissipi above the Illinois River, and if possible to its source.

"These two travelers left Fort Crevecœur February 28th, and, having entered the Misissipi, ascended it to about the 46° N. There they were arrested by a pretty high waterfall extending across the whole width of the river, and to which Father Hennepin gave the name of Falls of Saint Anthony of Padua. They then fell, by what accident I know not, into the hands of the Sioux, who retained them as prisoners for a considerable time, but did not maltreat them. They were at last delivered by some French who came from Canada.

"New troubles which befell M. de la Sale after the departure of Dacan and Father Hennepin, detained him at his Fort Crevecœur till the month of November, and then compelled him to return to Catarocouy. On his way he perceived on the Illinois River, which he was ascending, a site which seemed to him very adapted for the erection of a new fort. He traced the plan of one, called Mr. de Tonti, whom he appointed to build it, and continued his route. Scarcely had Tonti begun his work when he received information that the French whom he had left in Fort Crevecœur had revolted. He hastened back, but found only seven or eight men, the rest having deserted, with all they were able to carry.

"Soon after the Iroquois appeared, to the number of six hundred warriors, in sight of the Illinois settlements, and this irruption having increased the distrust of the Illinois against the French, the Chevalier de Tonti found himself in a strange embarrassment. The course which he adopted was to make himself a mediator between the two Indian nations, and in this negotiation he employed successfully the Recollect Fathers Gabriel de la Ribourde and Zenobius Membré, who had remained with him at Crevecœur. But the peace was not lasting, and the Iroquois, emboldened by the fear with which they seemed to be regarded, soon renewed their hostilities.

"Hitherto the Iroquois had not openly declared against the French: they at last undertook to drive them from the River of the Illinois, and the Chevalier de Tonti, having received information that an army of those Indians was coming to invest him in his Fort Crevecœur, did not consider it prudent to await their approach, and retired. Count de Frontenac, in his letter to the king . . . states that Tonti was pursued and wounded, and Father Gabriel de la Ribourde killed, by the Iroquois. He apparently was led to believe so from the first rumors, which almost always exaggerate bad tidings. The truth is that Tonti, not believing himself in a position to defend his fort against the Iroquois, evacuated it on the 11th of September, 1680, with five Frenchmen, who constituted his whole garrison, and the two Recollect Fathers whom I have already named, but he was not followed, or at least there was no action between him and the Iroquois.

"After ascending the Illinois River five leagues, he halted to dry his furs, and Father Gabriel having strayed a little into the woods while saying his breviary, was met by some Kicapous, who killed him, apparently in order to rob him. He was a holy religious, highly esteemed in New France for his virtue and moderation, and who had consulted his courage rather than his strength before attaching himself to an expedition, of which his age of seventy-one could not insure his seeing the close. This misfortune for some days delayed the march of the Chevalier de Tonti, who went to the bay of Lake Michigan to winter.

"M. de la Sale could not have been informed of this retreat, and he was greatly surprised when, early in the spring of the following year, he found no one at Fort Crevecœur on his reaching it. Having stationed a new garrison there, he dispatched men to work at a second fort, which he had traced the year before, and which was called Fort St. Louis. He then proceeded to Michillimakinac, where the Chevalier de Tonti had shortly before arrived with his party. They all set out from it together toward the end of August to proceed to Catarocouy, and after three months spent in running up and down to recruit a new body of Frenchmen and collect supplies, la Sale with his whole force took up his march for the Illinois, and there found his two forts in the position in which he had left them.

LA SALLE CHRISTENS THE COUNTRY LOUISIANA

"He descended the Illinois River, and on the 2d of February, 1682, he found himself on the Misissipi. On the 4th of March, with all the usual ceremonies, he took possession in form. This is all that is certainly known as to this voyage. . . .

"This important exploration thus completed, and the whole course of one of the greatest rivers in the world secured to France by acts of taking possession, to which no objection could be taken, la Sale re-embarked on the 11th of April. . . . On the 15th of May he fell sick, and detached the Chevalier de Tonti, with instructions to use all possible diligence to reach Michillimakinac. For his own part, he proceeded to spend part of the winter at the Bay, and did not reach Quebec till the spring of the ensuing year, 1683."

La Salle now returned to France, where he obtained from the king a patent making him commandant of this vast territory which he had named Louisiana.

THE ASSASSINATION OF LA SALLE
From Francis Parkman's *La Salle and the Discovery of the Great West*
Little, Brown & Company

Finally everything was ready, and on August 1, 1684, he sailed from France with a company of two hundred and eighty persons in four ships, to establish a colony in the land of his dreams. But Beaujeu, the navigator of the little squadron, lost his bearings and, instead of landing at the mouth of the Mississippi, anchored off Matagorda Bay in Texas. The colonists landed, but the ship containing most of the supplies was wrecked. Beaujeu soon after deserted La Salle, leaving him only one small vessel. La Salle built a fort, which he called St. Louis, and attempted to till the soil; but the Indians were hostile. By the end of the

FATHER HENNEPIN CELEBRATING MASS

From Parkman's *La Salle and the Discovery of the Great West*
Little, Brown & Company

[135]

year the little band, through disease, hardships, and Indian attacks, was reduced to less than forty souls.

Leaving half of them, including women and children, La Salle set out, at the beginning of 1688, to make his way to the Illinois. Among his party were his brother and two nephews. Privation, suffering, and discontent at length culminated in a conspiracy that resulted in the murder of La Salle's nephew; and when the brave explorer turned back to look for him, he himself met the same fate. Thus perished, May 20, 1687, at the hands of an assassin, the great La Salle, the bravest and most celebrated of those gallant French explorers who sought to establish an empire in the wilderness.

But the dream of La Salle was to come true in 1701 when another adventurous Frenchman set up a small trading station on the Detroit River—on the site which La Salle himself had visited thirty-one years before in his search for the Great River—and thus founded Detroit, one of the oldest cities on the American continent.

"Before Henry Hudson set foot on the island of Manhattan, and while Henry IV still sat on the throne of France," writes Edmund Kirke in "The City of the Strait," *Harper's Magazine*, August, 1886, "the Hurons pointed out the site whereon Detroit is built to Champlain, the founder of Quebec, as the natural gateway to 'the vast seas of sweet water,' and then was born in the brain of the great French navigator the dream of a 'New France,' which should extend from the Atlantic to the Pacific, and have Quebec and Detroit as its eastern and western fortresses.

"This dream was inherited by the French monarchs; but it was not till ninety years later that one of them attempted to make it a reality. Then Louis XIV commissioned the Sieur Antoine de la Mothe Cadillac, who from 1694 to 1699 had been in command at Mackinaw, to found at Detroit a settlement, and erect there a fort to hold the region of the Great Lakes for the French government. This was done; and Detroit, under the successive reigns of Henry IV, Louis XIII, XIV, and XV, was for nearly sixty years a French town—a bit of 'sunny France' hidden away in the heart of the western wilderness."

The Capitulation of Louisbourg

Illustration from
COLONIES AND NATION
by Woodrow Wilson

Originally published in
HARPER'S MAGAZINE, *June, 1901*

THE CAPITULATION OF LOUISBOURG AND THE FALL OF MONTCALM

Such it might have remained to this day had not the British under Amherst and Wolfe in August, 1758, forced the capitulation of Louisbourg—the strongest fortress in North America that stood a bulwark of defense for New France on Cape Breton's iron coast. But this great victory was only a step toward a greater one the following year when Wolfe changed the fate of North America by scaling the heights of Quebec and defeating the great Montcalm on the Plains of Abraham, the heroic Wolfe and the gallant Frenchman both

THE FALL OF MONTCALM

From Francis Parkman's *Montcalm and Wolfe.* Little, Brown & Company

[138]

dying from their wounds on the bloody field. "The surrender of Detroit," continues Kirke, "soon followed the conquest of Quebec; and then it became an English town, and the western headquarters of the British power in America. It so remained—the extreme outpost of western civilization—until July 11, 1796, when, in pursuance of the peace of 1783, it was quietly transferred to the United States.

"It was a sweltering day in July, 1701, when Cadillac, with his little fleet of birch-bark canoes, turned southwest from Lake St. Clair and entered the broad, clear, beautiful river now known as the Detroit. Had some native of the forest stood then upon its banks, he must have been lost in wonder at the unwonted spectacle of the strange flotilla. Twenty-five birchen boats—some measuring six feet wide and thirty-five feet long—gaudily decorated with Indian symbols and waving gayly the flags of France, glided gracefully down the stream to the exhilarating sounds of the fife and the drum, and the joyful shout that a long journey was over. The boats were manned by fifty soldiers in 'bright blue coats and white facings,' and carried four officers and fifty emigrants, with an abundant store of provisions and all the tools and utensils needed in the building and settling of a new town in the wilderness. Besides, there were on board two Roman Catholic priests, for, like all good Frenchmen, Cadillac had a tender concern for the souls of his people. He intended they should not neglect the mass, or forget their pater-noster. They had come a weary journey of forty-nine days, in those frail boats, over rough waves, the men bearing them on their shoulders on the long portage between the Ottawa River and Lake Huron, and it was but natural they should rejoice at the end of their voyage.

"Where the river leaves Lake Huron it is more than half a league in width, and broken by picturesque islands; but as it flows south-westward it contracts into a single channel and gradually narrows till at about ten miles' distance it has a breadth of only half a mile. This is the strait which was to give its name—Detroit—to both the river and the city to be built upon its northern bank. Here, at a sudden bend in the stream, the canoes were drawn up on the beach, and, landing, the voyagers ascended to a level plateau which rose by successive terraces to a height of about fifty feet above the bed of the river. . . .

THE LANDING OF CADILLAC

"Cadillac landed on the 24th of July, and by the close of the following month the chapel, the fort, and the dwellings of the settlers were erected, and the settlement had assumed all the order of an established community. Soon after this, Madame Cadillac, who had been left behind at Quebec, plunged into the wide wilderness to rejoin her husband. It was a thousand miles, in a birch-bark canoe, rowed by half-clad Indians or still more savage half-breeds, and the route was through a dense forest and over great seas swept by the September storms; but this brave woman undertook the journey attended by only a single female companion. When subsequently reminded of its hazards and hardships, she simply said, 'A woman who loves her husband as she should has no stronger attraction than his company, wherever he may be; everything else should be indifferent to her.' Cadillac has been censured for being 'often involved in troubles caused by his rashness and prejudices,' but whatever may have been his faults, he must have possessed noble traits of character to have inspired the strong devotion of such a woman.

"The adventurous Frenchman had now built a capital and assumed the governorship of a vast territory. His next step was to people his settlement and obtain the permanent good will of the natives of the Lake region. To these ends he resorted to the novel expedient of settling the Indians about him and encouraging his soldiers to marry their young women. In this way he hoped to augment his population and attach the aborigines to him by ties of kinship. The natives received his overtures kindly and before long four different tribes had established settlements within cannon-shot of the fort—the Miamis and Pottawatamies within half a mile on its either side, and the Hurons and Ottawas on the opposite side of the river, near the present town of Windsor. His scheme for

The Landing of Cadillac

Illustration from
THE CITY OF THE STRAIT
by Edmund Kirke

Originally published in
HARPER'S MAGAZINE, *August,* 1886

intermingling the white and red races was equally successful, for the Indian maiden soon learned to prefer Johnny Crapeau for a husband. He did not require her to plant his corn and dig his potatoes while he was away upon the hunt or lounging idly about the wigwam. Too highly civilized for that, he cultivated his own beets and cabbages, and arraying his dusky mate in gaudy gown and gewgaws, set her over his household to entertain his guests and preside as indoor divinity. . . .

"The settlement grew, and many came to it during the sixty years of French rule that followed. They brought their wives with them, and formed about the commandant a select society that gave a tone of cultivation to the better part of the white community. But in all these years the town was in a nebulous state—the nucleus French, the surrounding element a dusky barbarism. In the nature of things there could be no general and thorough amalgamation of these opposite elements, and consequently the town could not crystallize into a compacted community. But with the coming in of the English a new order of things was inaugurated. The Pontiac War soon followed, and that drove the savages from the suburbs. Then the people became more homogeneous, but the French were still an important element. They still retained their own language and religion, and they never affiliated cordially with the English, though the two nationalities had enough in common to make of each other friends and neighbors. It was no longer an attempt to marry civilization and barbarism, but an endeavor to make two white races not overmuch in love with each other dwell peaceably together in one household.

THE CONSPIRACY OF PONTIAC

"The Pontiac War was a crisis in the history of Detroit, and if tradition is to be trusted, the town was then saved from destruction by one of those romantic incidents that enliven the dull record of carnage which forms so large a portion of our Western annals. It was in 1763. Pontiac had formed the extensive coalition by which he hoped to drive the English back to the east of the Alle-

The Ojibway Maiden Disclosing Pontiac's Plot

Illustration from
THE CITY OF THE STRAIT
by Edmund Kirke

Originally published in
HARPER'S MAGAZINE, *August*, 1886

ghanies. Detroit was their western stronghold, and, that taken, his purpose would be half accomplished. The fort here was therefore fixed upon for the first attack, and the wily savage sought to capture it by stratagem.

"About three o'clock on the afternoon of May 1, 1763, Pontiac made a visit to the British commandant, Major Henry Gladwin, and proposed to him a council at the fort, to which he should come with some of his principal warriors, to smoke the pipe of peace and brighten the chain of friendship between his people and the English. Suspecting no treachery, the Englishman assented, and a date was fixed upon for the meeting. Before the appointed day arrived Gladwin was told that the Indians were borrowing saws and files from his blacksmith, and that some of them had been observed sawing off the ends of their rifle barrels. To this, though it was a singular circumstance, he gave but little thought, until it was explained to him on the day preceding the proposed council. Then a beautiful Ojibway maiden, who is said to have been enamored of Gladwin, came to his quarters, bringing a pair of moccasins she had at his request made from an elk skin he had furnished. He was much delighted with her beautiful workmanship, praised it highly, and requested her to make him another pair from the remainder of the peltry. She hesitated, but after a time took the skin and departed.

THE OJIBWAY MAIDEN DISCLOSES PONTIAC'S PLOT

"But she did not at once leave the fort. She lingered long about the entrance, as if uncertain whether to go or stay. . . . Quickly she turned and entered again the quarters of Gladwin. Holding out the pelt to him, she said, 'I cannot take it; I cannot make you the moccasins.'

"'Why not?' he asked. 'Why refuse me so small a favor?'

"'Because I may not be able to bring them to you,' she answered; and then, in reply to some further questions, she disclosed Pontiac's meditated treachery. Sixty of his bravest warriors had filed off the barrels of their rifles so they might be hidden under their blankets, and, thus armed, they would come to the council on the morrow. At a given signal from Pontiac they were to massacre the commandant, and then fall upon and slaughter the garrison, who, taken unarmed and unawares, would be able to make but feeble resistance. The knives had been already sharpened to take the scalps of the Englishmen. The warning of the Indian maiden was explicit, and only a fool stops his ears at the sound of danger. Gladwin had but a slender garrison of one hundred and thirty men, and Pontiac had two thousand warriors within the sound of his rifle. The odds were terrific; but the commandant did not shut his gates upon the savages. He met them, as Pontiac proposed, in friendly council; but was prepared to officiate, in case of treachery, at an extensive Indian funeral.

"On the following day—May 9, 1763—Pontiac came to the fort with sixty warriors, each having his blanket about him. Precisely at the hour appointed he entered the north gate and at the head of his warriors moved along a street lined on both sides with glittering ranks of redcoats, while at various points polished brass cannon glowered down upon him. At every corner he saw groups of fur traders, armed to the teeth, and every few seconds heard the measured tap of a drum, betokening warlike preparation. Astonished at the unexpected display, he was at first morose and silent; but after a few moments he turned to Gladwin and said, 'Why do I see so many of my father's young men standing in the streets with their guns?' He was told it was a custom of the English at the reception of distinguished guests; and then, stately and silent, he moved on to the council house.

"Here, his warriors seated in a circle about him, he rose and, holding in his hand a belt of wampum that was to have given the fatal signal, he made to Gladwin a fervid harangue, professing great friendship to the English. But he did not give the concerted signal, and he finally sat down amid the silent astonishment of his Indians. Then Gladwin approached him and, lifting the corner of his blanket, under which his rifle was concealed, charged him with his treachery, adding that this one breach of faith would be overlooked, but swift vengeance would follow another act of duplicity or aggression. The council then suddenly broke up, the Indians hastily retired, and the Pontiac War followed."

The Indians did not like it a bit when they saw the French leave and the English come to occupy the Ohio country back beyond the Alleghany Mountains. The French had treated them always as comrades and social equals, while now the English acted as though they meant to make slaves of them, occupying as they did so many posts in their country. Scarcely had the French left when settlers in large numbers began to pour over the mountains from Pennsylvania, Maryland, and Virginia. These settlers, mainly of Scotch-Irish extraction—stern and matter-of-fact, like all men of that stock—did not have much patience with the Indians; and as they advanced their settlement they drove the Indians farther and farther into the forest. Then, too, at this time a prophet appeared among the Indians and, preaching a crusade against the English, made it easy for Pontiac to form his conspiracy, the object of which was to drive the hated invaders from this Ohio country.

At length, all being ready, Pontiac struck the first blow in June, 1763; and in this war, which lasted nearly two years, Detroit, Niagara, and Fort Pitt were the only frontier posts that escaped the firebrand and the tomahawk. But before the end of 1765 the Indians were subdued and Pontiac himself was forced to sue for peace, although he remained hostile until his death in 1769.

Who these Scotch-Irish pioneers were—that adventurous, determined people who had already begun to cross the Alleghany Mountains while the French were yet making haste to occupy the valley of the Ohio and make themselves masters of its waterways before the English should gain a foothold there, we shall learn in the next chapter.

Chapter III

PIONEERS OF THE OLD WEST

HO were those people, whom we call the pioneers or backwoodsmen, who made the first settlements beyond the Alleghanies, subdued the western wilderness, and made it a fit habitation for civilized man— those fearless pathfinders, who blazed the way for the English occupancy of that vast territory known as the Ohio Valley, which the pioneers of France had won after great toil and hardship, and lost forever when Wolfe defeated Montcalm on the Plains of Abraham—that stalwart body of frontiersmen who for more than twenty-five years were constantly exposed to the assaults of bloodthirsty Indians, and, as they plowed their fields, had an armed sentry beside them?

For the answer we must return to the Europe of the middle

of the seventeenth century, when James I, seeking to heal the Irish sore, induced the lowland Scotch Presbyterians to plant colonies in the north of Ireland. There they prospered for more than two generations, but about 1704 and for many years following they fell under the royal displeasure, until finally, as the result of combined economic and religious oppression, they began to flock to America in large numbers.

Beginning in 1720, this migration continued for many years, until by the year 1770 the Scotch-Irish formed one third of the population of Pennsylvania. "Landing upon the seacoast all the way from Pennsylvania to the Carolinas and Georgia, this sturdy people . . . at once sought new and cheap lands"[1] which they found toward the frontier, "along the whole line of the Appalachian Mountains, at the backbone of the English colonies, extending eastward and westward and forming a prolific and influential element of the American people."[2]

Along with this migration of the Scotch-Irishmen went a considerable number of Germans who had come to America at about the same time; and there were also among them many of English, Welsh, and French-Huguenot stock. Together they formed a great frontier stream flowing westward to the free lands bordering the "Western Waters," until many of them at length reached the valleys of the Tennessee, the Cumberland, and the Watauga Rivers; there they made homes in the wilderness, where later grew up the great states of Kentucky and Tennessee.

These Scotch-Irish, then mingling with the descendants of many other races, whose fiber they greatly strengthened, became the pioneers of the American people in their march westward, and by their enterprising spirit won a new empire from the wilderness.

Among these pioneers, one of the most famous was Daniel Boone—backwoodsman, hunter, trader, cattle raiser, and farmer all in one, who in 1769 left his "family and peaceful habitation

[1] Thwaites, *France in America*, Amer. Nation, vol. vii, p. 148.
[2] Cheney, *European Background of American History*, Amer. Nation, vol. i, pp. 238-239.

A Kentucky Wedding

Illustration from
BUILDING THE NATION
by Charles Carleton Coffin

Harper & Brothers, 1883

on the Yadkin River in North Carolina, to wander through the wilderness of America in quest of the country of Kentucke."

With Boone on his trip in quest of the country of "Kentucke" went James Robertson, another heroic figure in the winning of the West. So struck were they with its beauty when they reached the valley of the Watauga, two thousand feet above the sea, that they returned two years later with some sixteen families and established the first permanent settlement in what is now the northeast corner of Tennessee. In 1772 they were "joined by John Sevier, who was 'well fitted for this wilderness work,' strong yet jovial, at once an Indian fighter, a statesman, and a gentleman," who, with Robertson, became the founder of the state of Tennessee. Under the leadership of these men, other settlements on the Watauga were combined under what was known as the Watauga Association. A civil government was set up with a self-imposed constitution, and thus was created an infant republic of the wilderness, the earliest example of "a government of the people, by the people," established by men of American parentage beyond the Alleghanies. This settlement was practically an independent colony, but in 1776, on petition of its leaders, it was placed under the jurisdiction of North Carolina.

THE BEGINNING OF NASHVILLE, TENNESSEE

In 1773 Boone guided a party of settlers beyond the Cumberland Mountains, but, being attacked by Indians, they were obliged to return to the settlements. Boone, however, continuing his exploring of the country, did not return until he had reached the rapids of the Ohio, a journey through the wilderness of over eight hundred miles. As a result of his explorations, pioneers were getting well established throughout the Cumberland Valley, and in 1780 Robertson led his followers from the Watauga to the region known as the French Lick. There he built a fort on the bluffs which, with a few log cabins, was the beginning of Nashville, the future capital of Tennessee. Their course from Watauga had been the circuitous one blazed by Boone through the woods of Kentucky, a distance of five hundred miles and a fifteen days' horseback journey.

Traveling in Frontier Days

Illustration from
THE CITY OF CLEVELAND
by Edmund Kirke

Originally published in
HARPER'S MAGAZINE, *March, 1886*

over a trail deep in snow. They were not molested by the Indians, and even took a few friendly savages with them as guides; but there was great suffering from the cold, for this particular winter was the most severe that had been known in a century.

This settlement, writes Howard Pyle in his article "On the Outposts," in *Harper's Magazine*, February, 1888, "was in the very heart of the wilderness, surrounded by nearly twenty thousand Creeks, Cherokees, Choctaws, and Chickasaws, all of whom were in alliance with Great Britain, which at that moment had overrun and all but subjugated the southern colonies."

In the spring of 1780 more settlers, including whole families, had come to Robertson's colony in the Cumberland Valley, until there were as many as five hundred scattered along the banks of the river, many of whom had come even from the coast which the British had occupied. Located in the very heart of the wilderness, they were too far away to look for aid from any neighbors. An association of the settlers on the lines of that of the Watauga Association was established by Robertson for the government of the colony, and the articles of the constitution adopted were signed by two hundred and fifty-six male citizens.

CAPTURE AND RESCUE OF BOONE'S DAUGHTER AND TWO GIRL COMPANIONS

Bloodthirsty attacks by the Indians were only too frequent and in these Indian outbreaks many of the settlers at a distance from the fort were found scalped and horribly mangled. So great was the death and havoc inflicted on the colony that many of the men were obliged to remove their women and children to places of safety in Kentucky, which, at that period, was better protected against the inroads of the savages. As an example of the bloody work that went on "It is enough to say that out of the two hundred and fifty-six men" who composed the colony, "thirty-seven, one by one, during sixty days, perished. In fact, during that entire year only one of the settlers died a natural death."

To return to Daniel Boone. As we have seen, he had blazed

Finding the Body of One of Their Companions,
Scalped and Horribly Mangled

Illustration from
ON THE OUTPOSTS—1780
by Howard Pyle

Originally published in
HARPER'S MAGAZINE, *February,* 1888

and cleared the way through the Kentucky woods which Robertson
and his colonists had followed. This road, known as the Wilderness

From *Harper's Magazine*, June, 1887

THE CAPTURE OF ELIZABETH AND FRANCES CALLOWAY

Road, was the route followed for many years by the pioneer farmers
in their march through the Great Valley to the desirable lands of

"Kentucke," and the thoroughfares that have supplied its place are still known by the same name. On his way he was attacked by Indians, but pushed on to the Kentucky River, where, on April 18, 1775, he built a fort which he called Boonesborough. This stockade served as a protection for Boone and his companions. It was also the meeting place for the members of the legislative body which the settlers chose to represent them. The little fort was in almost constant danger of attacks by Indians, and so near and real was this peril that in July, 1776, writes Drake in *Indian History for Young Folks*, "three young girls, one a daughter of Boone, the others daughters of Colonel Calloway, carelessly crossed the river opposite to Boonesborough in a canoe," and while "playing and splashing the water with their paddles" were seized and carried off by five Indians as the canoe drifted near the shore.

Pursuit of the Indians was taken up at daylight by Boone and eight other pioneers, among them three young men, the lovers of the girls. These experienced woodsmen soon found the trail taken by the Indians, which was marked by the elder Calloway girl's breaking twigs and bending bushes and dropping small bits which she tore from her dress as the Indians hurried them along. After following the trail for thirty miles, the pursuers overtook the Indians "as they were kindling a fire to cook their evening meal. Each party discovered the other at the same moment. Four of Boone's party fired, killing two of the Indians, and all immediately rushed in, in order to give them no time to murder the captives. The Indians fled, leaving guns, knives, and prisoners in their hasty flight. . . . The joy of the parents on thus discovering their lost darlings may be imagined; it cannot be described."

Early in 1778, Boone, while making salt at the Lower Blue Licks, was captured by the Indians and taken to Detroit, where Hamilton, the British commandant, treated him kindly. The Indians, refusing to give him up to the English, took him into the Shawnee country with them. While there Boone learned that Hamilton was gathering a force of warriors with which to attack the Kentucky settlements. Succeeding in making his escape, he reached Boonesborough in time to make ready its defense, and with about forty fighting men awaited the attack which he knew was about to be made. The Indians, under their leader, Duquesne, a former French officer, demanded the surrender of the fort. But Boone, standing upon one of the bastions, replied: "We are determined to defend our fort while a man is living, but we thank you for giving us notice and time to provide for our defense."

THE DEFENSE OF THE FORT AT BOONESBOROUGH

Duquesne not being oversanguine as to the success of his venture, then proposed that nine men be chosen from the garrison for the purpose of making a treaty which, when concluded, would terminate the siege and allow the return of the besiegers to their homes. This sounded good to Boone and he agreed to the proposal, only to discover that it was intended as a snare. A crowd of Indians immediately surrounded the nine men, and, under the "pretense of a friendly handshake at parting, two stout Indians grasped each of Boone's party." The sturdy woodsmen, however, instantly broke through the crowd of savages and gained the protection of the stockade. The siege then began and lasted for nine days and nights, the enemy finally giving it up on the tenth day and vanishing in the woods.

"Of the defenders of the fort," again quoting Drake, "one was killed and one wounded by a negro deserter who fired from the top of a neighboring tree. Boone, perceiving this, watched him and, when he saw his head, fired. The man was found after the battle with a ball in his head, the shot being made at the distance of one hundred and seventy-five yards. This was a feat worthy of the renowned Leather Stocking."

Having lost his lands in Kentucky in consequence of a defective title, Boone, still the pioneer and backwoodsman, went to the Missouri frontier in 1795, where he continued the occupations of hunter and trapper, again helping to make the wilderness a fit place for civilized man.

Another of these pioneer defenders of the frontier worthy of

Defense of the Station, Boonesborough

Illustration from
THE KENTUCKY PIONEERS
by John Mason Brown

Originally published in
HARPER'S MAGAZINE, *June,* 1887

mention was John Sevier, of Huguenot blood, whom we have already met with James Robertson establishing their republic on the Watauga in 1772. Moving farther east, just beyond the mountains of North Carolina, the Watauga Association had established another independent community at Jonesboro, where their town was built. A convention was held there, August 23, 1784, under the presidency of Sevier, which voted to declare the colony a separate state, due to North Carolina having voted to cede her western lands to the Confederation, thus intending to cast them off, they felt, from the parent state. They also endeavored to persuade the neighboring part of Virginia to join them. At this pass of affairs, the act of cession was repealed and Governor Martin appointed Sevier brigadier-general of the district, hoping that his influence would lead back the disaffected to their loyalty.

Sevier, however, did not succeed in persuading the Separatist leaders to give up their idea of independence. Ambitious men among them urged the people forward, and at a second convention, held December 14, 1784, they resolved to form a separate state, under the name of Franklin. A provisional government was formed of which Sevier was chosen governor, in March, 1785, whereupon the Governor of North Carolona was notified that the counties of Sullivan, Washington, and Greene were no longer a part of the state of North Carolina. Against the Separatists Governor Martin of North Carolina issued a manifesto, but the legislature of Franklin passed an act of oblivion as to all who should submit. The provisional constitution, based upon that of North Carolina, was adopted in November, 1785, as a permanent one, and the new state entered upon an independent career. Very soon, however, rivalries and jealousies arose among the leaders of the Separatists, and at length the Anti-Separatists, led by Colonel Tipton, Sevier's enemy, showed increasing strength, and now Franklin had two sets of officers, which condition of affairs threatened to bring on civil war. Finally an armed collision between men under Tipton and Sevier took place. Sevier's men were defeated, many of them being afterward arrested and taken to prison in irons. Sevier

[158]

The Woman Turned Fiercely Upon the Chieftain

In 1788 the boy Joseph Brown was captured by the Chicka-maugas. Joseph's captor was a young half-breed named Chia-chatt-alla, who spared his life that he might be the slave of his mother. But an Indian chieftain, fearing that when he grew older he would escape and pilot an army to destroy them all, demanded the boy's life. The woman, however, regardless in her fury of her personal safety, turned fiercely upon the chieftain, and so saved Joseph's life.

Illustration from
THE SOUTHERN GATEWAY TO THE ALLEGHANIES
by Edmund Kirke

Originally published in
HARPER'S MAGAZINE, *April, 1887*

himself met a similar fate, when, trusting to his popularity to save him, he came forth from his hiding place in the mountains.

Such excitement was never known beyond the Alleghanies as occurred when it was noised abroad the next morning that Sevier had been placed in irons and was to be tried on a charge of high

From *Harper's Magazine*, June, 1885

RESCUE OF SEVIER

treason, by the state authorities of North Carolina. "The tidings," as Edmund Kirke writes in "Knoxville in the Olden Time," *Harper's Magazine*, June, 1885, "had flown with the wind; men had come together as if by instinct, and before nightfall more than a thousand dauntless backwoodsmen, armed to the teeth, had gathered at Jonesboro, determined to rescue their beloved commander"—the

Joseph Brown Leading His Company to Nicojack, the Stronghold of the Chickamaugas

While a prisoner among these Indians he had discovered all their hiding places in the mountains, so that when the time came to take vengeance upon them for the murder of his father and two brothers, he was able to pilot an army through the trackless forest to their stronghold.

Illustration from
THE SOUTHERN GATEWAY TO THE ALLEGHANIES
by Edmund Kirke

Originally published in
HARPER'S MAGAZINE, *April,* 1887

man who for years, without pay or reward, "had stood sentinel over their homes, had guarded them through terrible dangers, and led them to wonderful victories" over the Indians. It seemed for a time that there would be a hostile invasion of the mother state to effect his release, but, finally, more moderate counsels prevailed. Nothing better serves to illustrate the people's devotion to him, as well as to show us a picture of the arduous life of those times, than his ingenious and dramatic rescue by a party headed by one of his lieutenants, James Cosby.

With three others—Major Evans, and James and John Sevier, the two sons of the general—Cosby proposed to go to Morganton, where the trial was in progress, and to effect by stratagem what it would have been hazardous to undertake by open force. Accordingly, the rescuers proceeded to Morganton on horseback, "leading" Mr. Kirke says, "a mare of Sevier's which was known as the swiftest-footed animal in the territory. The rescuers halted on the outskirts of Morganton and, concealing their horses in a clump of underbrush, left them there in charge of the young Seviers. Then Cosby and Evans, disguised as countrymen, entered the town. When they arrived at the courthouse Evans dismounted and, throwing the bridle loosely over the neck of the animal, stood with her directly before the open door and in plain view of the interior of the building. Then Cosby entered the courtroom and, elbowing his way up the crowded aisle, halted directly in front of the judge's bench and only a few feet from where his beloved leader stood encompassed by the court officials. Catching his eye, Cosby, by a significant gesture, directed Sevier's attention to his horse, that stood at the door. At one glance the quick eye of Sevier took in the situation. Seeing that he was understood, Cosby pressed closer to the bench and in quick, energetic tones said to the judge, 'Are you not about done with that man?' The question, and the tone and manner of the speaker, drew all eyes upon him in amazement. For a few moments—as Cosby had intended—all was confusion. Taking advantage of this, Sevier sprang from among the officers and with two bounds he was upon the back of his horse,

"The Cherokees Are Coming"

Illustration from
KNOXVILLE IN THE OLDEN TIME
by Edmund Kirke

Originally published in
HARPER'S MAGAZINE, *June*, 1885

and in two hours far away in the mountains. As the news of Sevier's escape flew from hamlet to hamlet, the whole territory broke out into a blaze of bonfires and illuminations, and soon the people elected him—branded rebel and outlaw as he was—to the senate of North Carolina, and within twelve months Washington gave him the rank of general, with supreme military command of the district now comprised in East Tennessee."

Sevier thus stands out as one of the most prominent and picturesque figures in the early pioneering days of Tennessee. He was called "the greatest of Indian fighters," having fought against the savage Creeks, Chocktaws, and Cherokees—the most warlike of all the native tribes east of the Mississippi. He was their Nemesis, and when, as only too often happened, a horseman came riding in hot haste into some quiet town on the border, crying out, "The Cherokees are coming!" "Nolichucky Jack," as Sevier was belovedly called, did not fly to the protection of the fort, but, at the head of other renowned Indian fighters, was soon close at the heels of the savages, driving them to their mountain fastnesses and carrying havoc and fire to scores of Cherokee villages.

But for their strong, rude log forts and the untiring vigilance of such men as Sevier, the settlers, so constantly menaced by the inroads of the savages, would have been exterminated. And so the sterling honesty and high soldierly qualities of this most attractive of men won him the admiration and affection of all the border people.

In 1796, when Tennessee was admitted to statehood the people elected him their governor, which office, through re-election, he held for six terms—until 1810—and the year following he was sent to represent his state in Congress.

Another of the group of these defenders of the frontier was George Rogers Clark, who, early in 1774, when he was but twenty-one years of age, came to settle in the country of "Kentucke" which Boone had explored in 1769. In this territory there were no permanent Indian settlements, the Ohio Indians having reserved these lands as their common hunting and fighting grounds. Due to the influx of settlers on these lands, and to the murder by some lawless whites of the family of Logan, chief of the Mingos, a fierce Indian war broke out shortly after the arrival of Clark from Virginia.

In the war which followed Clark was in command of a company. Other frontiersmen, among them Evan Shelby, brother of Isaac Shelby, the first Governor of Kentucky, and James Robertson, founder of Tennessee, also took a prominent part. This outbreak is known as "Dunmore's War," because it was conducted under the directions of Governor Dunmore of Virginia. It ended October 10th, 1774, at Point Pleasant, on the Great Kanawha, resulting in the complete defeat of the Shawnee Indians under Chief Cornstalk. Not only were the lands of the Kentucky and Tennessee region now opened for the inrush of more settlers by the spirit of these daring frontiersmen, but Virginia also was able to establish her hold upon the country between the mountains and the Ohio, as to the ownership of which she was in dispute with Pennsylvania.

Clark's greatest achievement, however, was made in 1777, when his genius foresaw the importance of conquering for the new republic the "Illinois country" which England then controlled by her possession of forts at Kaskaskia, and Cahokia on the Mississippi, and Vincennes on the Wabash, which also served as rallying points from which Indian raids were made on the settlements.

Patrick Henry, now Governor of Virginia, approved Clark's scheme for capturing the British posts, and in May, 1778, he was ready. "He took," says Wilson, "but one hundred and eighty picked riflemen, a modest flotilla of small boats, and a few light pieces of artillery, but they sufficed. Before the summer was out he had gained easy mastery of the little settlements which lay to the northward upon the Mississippi and within the nearer valley of the Wabash. . . .

"When the winter came Colonel Hamilton, the British commander at Detroit, came south into the forest with a motley force of five hundred men, mixed of regulars, Tories, and Indians . . .

[165]

and occupied Vincennes again, upon the Wabash; but Clark struck once more, sending his boats up the river and bringing his picked force straight across the frozen forests from Kaskaskia by the Mississippi; and by the end of February, 1779, Colonel Hamilton and all his levy were his prisoners. The Illinois country was added to Virginia, and the grant of her ancient charter 'up into the land, west and northwest' seemed made good again by the daring of her frontiersmen."

"Few events," says Van Tyne in his *American Revolution*, "have had a vaster influence upon the future of the nation than this expedition of Clark's. Not only did he secure the western gate of the Republic, but he gained these western lands, the ownership of which greatly advanced the idea of union, since there was a possession in which all of the states were interested."

Due, therefore, to the westward advance of these daring frontiersmen, new conditions of life arose, which in turn developed political, economic, and social problems, the solution of which has occupied the American people even up to the present day. In the beginning, the wilderness mastered the early comers, but by and by these sturdy men mastered the wilderness, and, in doing so, a transformation took place, for behold a new people was created—a people peculiarly American, more so than their kindred of the older coast towns, who had been developing their lives and institutions on lines more or less European. Out of touch with their brethren of the lowlands, our backwoodsmen were left free to work out their own salvation on independent, American lines. "There, among these men," says Van Tyne, "economic equality begot social equality, and political equality and democracy followed." There, truly, the title to manhood was the title to citizenship; there, too, were reborn the purposes and ideals of democracy and individualism which before and since their time have been characteristic of the American spirit and made the meaning of America what it is to all who have come within her influence. Nothing helped more in the formation of the American spirit than the character these pioneers showed themselves to be possessed of—strong enough to obey self-imposed laws.

Part III
The Nation

Chapter 1

RUMBLINGS OF THE STORM

XACTLY one hundred years before the thirteen Colonies declared their independence of Great Britain, July 4, 1776, it will be remembered that there occurred in Virginia a great outburst of popular discontent, known as Bacon's Rebellion. Although the immediate cause of the trouble was a war between the Colonists and the Indians, at bottom the rebellion was a protest against the misrule of Sir William Berkeley, the royal governor of Charles II, and the renewed enforcement of the Navigation Acts, the operation of which caused great distress to the Colonists by greatly lowering the price of tobacco and correspondingly raising the price of all European goods sold to the Colonists by English merchants.

Many writers have compared Bacon's Rebellion to that which resulted one hundred years later in the American Revolution. Without, however, going as far as this, we are justified in saying that the putting in operation of the Navigation Acts and the other restrictive laws of trade, which were made more and more stringent in the years that followed, had more to do with alienating the Colonists and preparing them for the final break with the mother country than all the other measures combined which had been adopted to render the Colonies subjective dependencies of the British crown.

[169]

From the very beginning England found great difficulty in enforcing these laws. They were evaded in all the Colonies, and especially in Massachusetts, where they weighed most heavily upon the people; and the failure of Massachusetts to obey these regulations, as well as her general independent attitude toward the crown in other matters, caused her charter to be annulled in 1684. This was followed by the "tyranny of Andros," who ruled Massachusetts as a conquered province until April, 1689. In that year he himself was overthrown and imprisoned as the result of the "Glorious Revolution" which made William and Mary king and queen of England.

Beginning with the reign of William III, Massachusetts, like each of the other Colonies except Rhode Island and Connecticut, was ruled by a governor appointed by the British government. During the seventy-odd years that elapsed between the accession of William and Mary and the Treaty of Paris in 1763, by the terms of which France was expelled from North America, the mother country took care that the constant bickerings that were going on during these years between the Colonists and the representatives of the crown should not become serious enough to cause a rupture in the generally peaceful relations that prevailed. With but short intervals, these were years of war between France and England; and as there was a New France in America, powerful of itself and rendered more so by alliance with the Indian tribes, hostilities between the two nations in Europe necessarily meant a war between their colonies in the New World. In these circumstances, it certainly was the part of wisdom for England to cease for the time being all repressive acts against the Colonies, whose loyalty and support were so necessary, if victory were finally to perch on England's banner in her long and difficult half century of conflict with France, in which the stake was the possession of a continent in America and maritime and commercial ascendancy in Europe. The last act in the long series of Colonial wars of the eighteenth century had its beginning in America in 1753, when Governor Dinwiddie sent George Washington, then a young man of twenty-one years

Washington's Retreat from Great Meadows

Illustration from
COLONEL WASHINGTON
by Woodrow Wilson

Originally published in
HARPER'S MAGAZINE, *March*, 1896

of age, to warn the French away from Fort Le Bœuf, which was in territory that Virginia claimed as belonging to the British crown. The French, however, paid no heed to the warning, and in the spring of the following year it proved to be only a step toward making themselves masters of the fort which the English had built at the forks of the Ohio where the present city of Pittsburgh stands.

WASHINGTON'S RETREAT FROM THE GREAT MEADOWS

Meanwhile Washington was on his way to reinforce the fort with a force of backwoodsmen when he learned that it was held by the French, who had named it Duquesne in honor of the governor of Canada. As Washington proceeded he came in contact with a small French force under M. Jumonville, and in a surprise attack not far from his camp in the Great Meadow the French commander was killed and the whole detachment captured. News of this reverse quickly brought a large French force to attack Washington in his rude intrenchment upon the Great Meadows. A stubborn defense was maintained, but, being greatly outnumbered, Washington was forced to retire, leaving the disputed territory in the hands of the French.

But early in June of the following year Washington was once more to take part in an attack on Fort Duquesne—this time as a member of the staff of General Braddock, who came from England early in 1755 with his regiments of redcoats to act as chief commander of all the British troops in America. Braddock led two thousand men into the wilderness, following the route Washington had taken to the Great Meadows. In spite of Washington's advice to disregard the rules of European war in this campaign in the wilderness, this arrogant and indiscreet general, after entering the trail which led to the fort, with two thousand men, including five hundred Virginians and fourteen hundred regulars, besides two independent companies from New York, struck into the wilderness, confident that ere long Fort Duquesne would be in his hands. And so it would have been, Braddock's force being greatly superior to that of the French, had he followed the advice of Washington and

The Burial of Braddock

Illustration from
COLONEL WASHINGTON
by Woodrow Wilson

Originally published in
HARPER'S MAGAZINE, *March*, 1896

adopted the backwoodsman fashion of fighting. But he was a fanatic on military rules, and, deaf to all advice from the provincials, he led his men in close formation along the forest road, now lined with French and Indian foes. Thus he pushed forward in blind confidence to his fate, and as he marched along the trail leading to the fort a murderous fire was poured into the advancing column by the French and their Indian allies ambushed in two ravines that lined both sides of the trail. Panic immediately broke out among the regulars as they saw scores shot down by the unseen enemy, who, firing from the protection of the trees and rocks behind which they lurked, found in the brilliant color of the British uniform a sure target for their expert aim. Braddock himself fought bravely until he, too, received a mortal wound and was carried off the field by Washington's provincials. Three days later he died and was buried in a forest grave.

Two horses had been shot under Washington, but he himself escaped unhurt—saved for greater things. The defeat was no fault of his or of the Virginians, whose courage and steadiness throughout the action were beyond praise. After Washington's retreat from the Great Meadows the Virginia Assembly had voted a fund for the equipment of the new companies of militia, each to have its own commander, with no officer higher than captain. Feeling that this had been done by Governor Dinwiddie mainly to belittle himself, Washington had at once resigned and sought a place on the staff of General Braddock.

WASHINGTON AND MARY PHILIPSE

Determined to have it settled as to who should now have the chief command in Virginia, Washington traveled to Boston to consult Governor Shirley, who had become acting commander-in-chief of the Colonial forces. In the course of his journey he was given many receptions, for his campaigns against the French in the Ohio Valley were everywhere known. While in New York he stayed with his friend, Beverley Robinson, and there met Mary Philipse, a beautiful heiress, also a guest, and the sister of Mrs.

Washington and Mary Philipse

Illustration from
COLONEL WASHINGTON
by Woodrow Wilson

Originally published in
HARPER'S MAGAZINE, *March,* 1896

Robinson. Washington lost his heart to this beauty and wanted to marry her. Love making, however, must give way to duty, and, Governor Shirley having restored him to his former rank, Washington hastened back to Virginia to take up the task that confronted him—the defense of a desolate forest frontier of more than three hundred miles, now threatened by the tomahawk and scalping knife.

Thus began in 1754 the war known in Europe as the Seven Years' War, and in America as the French and Indian War. In this war England, by the aid of her American colonies, was the victor, while vanquished France, in accordance with the stipulations of the Peace of Paris of 1763, retired from the continent of North America.

In 1760, three years before the Peace of Paris, George III became King of England. From the time of William III (1688) it had become an established principle for the sovereign to rule through responsible ministers with seats in Parliament, but in George III England was to have a king whose object was to restore to the monarchy the power which the kings had wielded in the state in the old days. George III believed that a king should govern as well as rule, and he resolved to be such a king. He also believed that the Colonies were politically mere "dependencies" and economically "possessions" belonging to the crown; as such they should be taxed and made subject to the authority of Parliament. To accomplish this twofold aim he proceeded to cause the fall of the old Whig aristocracy which had controlled the government of England for almost half a century. This purpose he achieved by calling to office inferior men who would do his bidding. Most important among such men was Lord North, leader of the new Tory party of "king's friends," who became premier in January, 1770. In the name of this faithful servant, ever ready to do his master's bidding, George III tried the experiment of governing as well as reigning for the next twelve years—until the surrender of Cornwallis at Yorktown finally made it clear to this stubborn king that in attempting to make the Colonies subject to the authority of Parliament and him-

Christmas Morning in Old New York Before the Revolution

By the magic power of the imagination, after a careful study of old prints, old costumes, and old records, Mr. Pyle has recalled the life of the past and given us a picture of New York as it appeared in good old Colony times. There are the old taverns and warehouses, the groups of soldiers and citizens, just as we may fancy they appeared in the days when the patriots were beginning to scheme for liberty and independence.

Illustration from
HARPER'S WEEKLY

Originally published
December 25, 1880

self supreme over the Parliament, he had only succeeded in losing America.

During the half century of the French and Indian wars England had made no serious effort to enforce the Acts of Navigation and trade. Not, however, because of any liberality on the part of the British government, but rather to avoid irritating the Colonies, whose loyalty and support were so essential in the struggle to drive New France from America. However, with the ending in 1763 of the French and Indian War, and with the menace from France forever removed, the British ministers chose this time, above all others, for the rigid enforcement of the laws of trade that had remained a dead letter for so many years.

To these ill-advised measures for increasing the king's revenue George III also proposed to lay taxes on the Colonies for the support of the British army which was to be retained in America to protect the Colonists against possible attacks from the Indians. This revenue would also become the source of a new fund for the payment of the salaries of the royal governors and of the other officials whom the king was to appoint to carry out his new policy. Moreover, these important officials of the crown would thereby be independent of the Colonial legislatures—a fact of the utmost importance to George III.

Furthermore, the time was even more ill chosen for putting them into effect. The time was the years immediately following the close of the French and Indian War, toward the winning of which the Colonial levies of some twenty-five thousand well-equipped troops had done so much, and in which the men from the thirteen Colonies had fought side by side, and from the contact, came to realize that they were somehow very much alike—different from their British comrades in arms—no longer simply men from Massachusetts, Pennsylvania, and Virginia, but Americans all. At that moment, although the Colonists did not realize it, the American nation was born and the long conflict between them and the mother country had its inception.

In 1765 nobody in England regarded it as unjust to collect

taxes from the Colonies to support an army for its own defense and to defray the expenses incurred by the crown in administering Colonial affairs. As regards the necessity of preserving and advancing the bounds of the British Empire, the people on both sides

From *Harper's Magazine*, August, 1883

AN OUT-OF-DOOR TEA PARTY IN COLONIAL NEW ENGLAND

of the Atlantic were agreed; "but," as Carl Becker says in *The United States, An Experiment in Democracy*, "they differed radically in their ideas of how the Empire ought to be organized and governed, and it is this difference which explains why" the British "thought the Stamp Act just and reasonable," while the Americans "thought it unjust and unreasonable.

"In the eighteenth century," continues Becker, "English government, and to a large extent English opinion in political matters, was controlled by a fairly small and a fairly selfish land owning and commercial oligarchy; and the complacence and egoism of this oligarchy were never greater than just after the Seven Years' War, when

From *Harper's Magazine*, March, 1882

THE PRESS GANG IN NEW YORK

all the world was fearing or admiring the tremendous success of Great Britain. Naturally enough, therefore, the average Englishman felt that this Empire was the result of the virtues and the sacrifices of England, and that as it had been created so it must necessarily be held together by the force of British arms and of British laws. . . . What could be more reasonable, therefore, than to suppose that the defense and the development of the Empire must be undertaken by the only supreme power there was—namely the British Parliament? . . .

"The American Colonists regarded the Empire in a somewhat different light. They knew very well, what the Englishman was likely to forget, that in the seventeenth century the Colonies had been established without much aid from England, in some cases by people who had been driven out of England in order to escape religious or political oppression. The Americans felt also that the new interest in the Colonies which the English government was now exhibiting was due to the fact that the trade of the

From *Harper's Magazine*, March, 1882

ISAAC SEARS ADDRESSING THE MOB

Colonies was becoming supremely important to the commercial and landowning aristocracy of England. . . . The Americans felt that whatever importance the American Colonies had as parts of the Empire, whatever economic or military or political value they possessed, was due to the labor and the sacrifices of the Colonists themselves, who, therefore, deserved quite as much credit for building up the wonderful British Empire as the people of England.

"The fundamental notion of Americans was admirably expressed by Benjamin Franklin in 1755:

"'British subjects, by removing to America, cultivating a wilderness, extending the domain, and increasing the wealth, commerce, and power of the mother country, at the hazard of their lives and fortunes, ought not, and in fact do not, thereby lose their native rights.'

"By their native rights Americans meant the traditional right of Englishmen to govern and tax themselves in assemblies of their own choosing. Englishmen had such an assembly in Parliament, but the Colonies were not, and in the nature of the case could not well be, represented in Parliament; but they had now, and had always had, their own assemblies, by which they had hitherto governed and taxed themselves. . . . It was through these assemblies that they had raised the money to support the Empire in the last war against France, and they were quite willing in the future to raise their fair share of taxes for the support of the Empire; but they wished to raise these taxes through their own assemblies in their own way. If the Parliament could levy and collect a Stamp Tax, it could levy and collect any and all taxes, and it could regulate the powers of the Colonial assemblies or abolish them altogether. The right of Parliament to tax the Colonies, in fact, involved the right to abolish colonial self-government; and fundamentally, therefore, the Colonies were contending for the right of self-government.

"In defense of this right the Colonists resisted the Stamp Tax. All classes refused to use the stamped papers; in many cases the stamps were destroyed by mobs."

A Committee of Patriots Delivering an Ultimatum
to a King's Councilor

Illustration from
A SIGN FROM HEAVEN
by Basil King

Originally published in
HARPER'S MAGAZINE, *January,* 1908

Rumblings of the Storm

Secret organizations known as the "Sons of Liberty" now sprang up in all the Colonies and at once offered forcible resistance to the execution of the obnoxious law. Riots first broke out in Boston, where the effigy of Andrew Oliver, one of the stamp collectors, was suspended, with that of Lord Bute, from an elm tree, known thereafter as the "Liberty Tree." In New York the Sons of Liberty undertook to enforce nonimportation agreements and to force the

From *Harper's Magazine*, March, 1882

THE MOB ATTEMPTING TO FORCE A STAMP OFFICER TO RESIGN

stamp officers to resign, as had been done in Boston. One of the many committees met at the Province Arms Coffee House and agreed that no goods should be imported from Great Britain until the act was repealed. Citizens paraded through the streets and burned the effigy of Governor Colden as the Boston people had burned that of Oliver's. The following day, when a paper was read from the balcony of the Province Arms calling upon the people to suppress riots, Isaac Sears, an old privateersman, addressing the mob that had gathered, advised them that this call was merely an attempt to prevent their getting possession of the stamps. Order was not restored until several days later, when the stamps were surrendered.

BROWNEJOHN'S WHARF

The next year the enforcement of the Townshend duties brought British frigates to Boston and New York. Press gangs from these ships often operated in the water-front streets of both cities, and spared neither friend nor foe when sailors were wanted. It might be the fate of any citizen to be kidnaped by these lawless gangs, but privateersmen were most sought after, and, when found, were seized and impressed with the greatest glee. In Boston further attempts at the kidnaping of peaceful citizens by crews from the frigate caused riots to break out. As a result a town meeting was held immediately afterward and a petition was drawn up demanding of the governor the instant removal of the offending man-of-war from the harbor. The practice of pressing sailors and citizens into service had often occurred in previous years of peace, and was one of the chief causes of the War of 1812. During the Revolution, however, the press gangs did not have much opportunity to ply their trade. During that period when the British were in occupation at New York, her captains, when in need of sailors to help prey on the commerce of the patriots, resorted to the more gentle method of recruiting the privateersmen who frequented the taverns along the water front, such as the King's Head on Brownejohn's wharf.

"Partly on account of opposition in the Colonies, partly on account of the pressure from English merchants who complained that their business was being ruined," says Becker, "the Stamp Act was repealed in 1776. But the next year, after a change of Ministry, certain duties known as the Townshend duties were laid on the importation of tea, glass, painters' colors, and paper. The Colonists had claimed that the Stamp Tax was unconstitutional because it was an 'internal' tax; but now they abandoned the distinction between internal and external taxes and objected to the levying of any taxes whatever, including import duties intended to

Brownejohn's Wharf, New York

*Here in the King's Head Tavern was set up a recruiting station
to obtain sailors for the British frigates.*

Illustration from
OLD NEW YORK TAVERNS
by John Austin Stevens

Originally published in
HARPER'S MAGAZINE, *May*, 1890

raise a revenue. After three years of controversy and strife, of rioting and of restrictive nonimportation agreements, the British government again yielded and repealed all of the duties save the threepenny duty on tea, which was maintained, not for the revenue which it would bring in, but as an assertion of the right of Parliament to levy taxes on the Colonies.

THE BOSTON TEA PARTY

"Although the Colonies insisted that the duty on tea was unconstitutional, the controversy largely subsided" until 1773, when the East India Company "sent over four cargoes of tea billed to the four ports of Boston, New York, Philadelphia, and Charleston. The Boston shipment arrived first, in the fall of 1773, but when it was attempted to land the tea, a crowd of men disguised as Indians boarded the ship and threw the tea into the harbor. In New York and Philadelphia the tea was sent back to England, and at Charleston it was stored in the basement of the custom-house. In reply to these acts, particularly to the destruction of the tea at Boston, the British government decided to make a final test of the authority of Parliament. By overwhelming majorities the Parliament passed what were known as the Coercive Acts, one of which suspended the Massachusetts government and placed the Colony under military rule, while another closed the port of Boston until the town should make compensation to the East India Company for the loss of its property."

AN ULTIMATUM TO A KING'S COUNCILOR

Another of the Coercive Acts was the statute known as the Regulation Act which provided that members of the council were to be appointed by the king and to hold office during his pleasure; all the judges, sheriffs, and other court officers were to be appointed in like manner and their salaries paid by the crown; and, as in the case of the councilors, such officers could be removed only by the king. The people of Boston rose in violent protest against these arbitrary measures, and the circular letters which they sent to the other Colonies asking for support were met with prompt and em-

The Boston Tea Party

Illustration from
COLONIES AND NATION
by Woodrow Wilson

Originally published in
HARPER'S MAGAZINE, *August,* 1901

phatic response to co-operate with Massachusetts in whatever measures she should adopt to prevent their execution, all the other Colonies realizing that the treatment accorded to Boston would shortly be visited upon themselves. Meetings were accordingly held throughout the Colonies, the final result of which was the call for a Continental Congress to meet in Philadelphia. But before the Congress had time to assemble, Massachusetts assumed an attitude of defiance against the Regulation Act under which the people had resolved that no government should be set up. Around the courthouses crowds gathered to prevent the judges from sitting, jurors refused to be sworn, and many of the governor's councilors were forced to resign. Those officers who resisted the demands of the patriots to surrender their commissions were reviled and treated with contempt by the populace. Among these "king's councilors" was one of Boston's most honored and formerly popular citizens, whose strong Tory inclinations would not allow him to refuse to serve his sovereign. Whereupon a committee of patriots—his old neighbors—went to his house and there, in the presence of his wife and daughter, delivered an ultimatum—that either he must give up his membership in the council or else they—his life-long friends and associates, as well as all other patriots in the Colony—would refuse to hold intercourse with him or any that dwelt beneath his roof.

It was natural that there should be many men of this type among the conservative class—men to whom revolution meant not only disloyalty to their king, but also the rending of family and national ties by the breaking up of the established social order.

Tory Refugees on Their Way to Canada

Illustration from
COLONIES AND NATION
by Woodrow Wilson

Originally published in
HARPER'S MAGAZINE, *December,* 1901

The majority of those who held these views were not to be found in New England, but rather in New York and Pennsylvania, where the non-English element formed a considerable part of the population; and especially in New York which had been for many years the chief center of the royalist government in America. Next to the crown officers there, the clergy and the college presidents, like Cooper of King's College, formed the backbone of this party; and naturally many of the students there, and in the other Colonial institutions as well, became their strong adherents.

When, however, the Declaration of Independence compelled men to publicly declare themselves, there were many bitter political discussions, and the loyalists, feeling themselves proscribed on account of their opinions, began to seek places of refuge outside the Colonies. Those who remained had the alternative of odious restraint at home or banishment. To a large proportion exile was preferable to imprisonment, and hundreds abandoned their country and fled to Nova Scotia or to England; while many of the young men among them joined the British forces and took up arms against their radical countrymen.

In spite of their strong loyalist president and teachers, however, the majority of the students at King's College before very long took the side of the patriots.

STUDENT DAYS OF ALEXANDER HAMILTON—1774

Among the students of this institution, which afterward became Columbia University, was Alexander Hamilton, who there began the remarkable career which was to be so important in determining the course of his country's history.

The Rev. Dr. Samuel Johnson, being considered an expert in starting colleges, having been first tutor of Yale College when it was established at New Haven, became its first president in the year 1754. In that first year, on the 17th of July, "the worthy president might have been seen in the vestryroom in the schoolhouse attached to Trinity Church, teaching the eight students who

A Political Discussion

Illustration from
COLONIES AND NATION
by Woodrow Wilson
Originally published in
HARPER'S MAGAZINE, *December*, 1901

then constituted King's College. Their names were Samuel Ver-
planck, Rudolph Ritzema, Philip Van Cortlandt, Robert Bayard,
Samuel Provoost, Thomas Marston, Henry Cruger, and Joshua
Bloomer."

From *Harper's Magazine*, October, 1884

PRESIDENT JOHNSON OF KING'S COLLEGE TEACHING HIS FIRST CLASS

Doctor Johnson was succeeded in the presidency in 1763 by the
Rev. Myles Cooper, who came from Queen's College, Oxford, of
which he was a fellow; and was still the president, eleven years
later, when Alexander Hamilton entered—considered to have been

Alexander Hamilton Addressing the Mob

Illustration from
KING'S COLLEGE
by John McMullen

Originally published in
HARPER'S MAGAZINE, *October*, 1884

the most distinguished student that King's College ever had. "At that time," to quote from an article on King's College in *Harper's Magazine* for June, 1885, "all men's minds were deeply moved by the great question of the Revolution. President Cooper sided with the mother country, talking and writing with all his power against the freedom of the Colonies. The tide of indignation rising higher and higher against such doctrines, it was finally determined to hold a public meeting in the open fields just above Dey Street, on the 6th of July, 1774, for the purpose of protesting against the acts of the authorities.

"Young Hamilton was urged to address the meeting, and as he closed a brilliant and impassioned address the cry of surprise, 'It is a collegian,' with which his youthful appearance was received gave way to loud expressions of wonder and applause.

"Young Hamilton presently crossed swords, or pens, with his college president, who could not believe at first that so young a man could be so strong a pamphleteer. In one of the periods of the excitement a liberty mob approached the college with the purpose of laying violent hands on the Tory president. As they drew near his residence, Hamilton and Robert Troup, a fellow student, ascended the steps, and, fearful lest in this moment of irritation they might commit some excess, Hamilton, in order to give the president time to escape, harangued the mob with great eloquence and animation 'on the excessive impropriety of their conduct and the disgrace they were bringing on the cause of liberty.'

"While Hamilton was holding the crowd by his eloquence, another student had informed the president of his danger, barely in time to enable him to escape, half dressed, over the college fence. Reaching the shore of the Hudson, he finally took refuge in the house of a friend, whence, during the following night, he boarded the *Kingfisher*, an English ship of war, in which shortly afterward he sailed for England."

To quote from *The United States, An Experiment in Democracy:* "As the king truly said upon the passage of the Coercive Acts, 'The

After the Massacre

Samuel Adams demanding of Governor Hutchinson the Instant
Withdrawal of British Troops

Illustration from
COLONIES AND NATION
by Woodrow Wilson

Originally published in
HARPER'S MAGAZINE, *August,* 1901

die is now cast; the Colonists must either submit or win complete independence.' Nothing was more true, "and, now that the issue

From *Harper's Magazine*, August, 1883

THE "BOSTON MASSACRE"

was so clearly one of legislative independence and not merely one of taxation, the Colonists gradually changed their argument once more

[196]

Burning of the "Gaspee"

Illustration from
COLONIES AND NATION
by Woodrow Wilson

Originally published in
HARPER'S MAGAZINE, *August*, 1901

and from this time on were inclined to deny not merely the right of Parliament to tax the Colonies, but the right of Parliament to legislate for them at all."

"The taxes," writes Wilson in his *History of the American People*, "had yielded nothing; the single tax on tea would serve to assert a right without the rest. Meanwhile a very ominous thing had happened in Boston—though the Ministers had not yet heard of it when the bill passed to repeal the taxes. Upon an evening in March, 1770, a mob had attacked a squad of the king's redcoats in King Street, pelting them with sharp pieces of ice and whatever else they could lay their hands on, and daring them derisively to fire; and the troops had fired, being hard pressed and maddened. Five of the mob were killed and six wounded, and a thrill of indignation and horror went through the excited town. The next day a great meeting in Faneuil Hall sent a committee to Mr. Hutchinson, the governor, to demand the instant withdrawal of the troops. Samuel Adams headed the committee, imperious and on fire; told the governor, in the council chamber where they met, that he spoke in the name of three thousand freemen who counted upon being heeded; and won his point. The troops were withdrawn to an island in the bay. The town had hated their 'lobster backs' for all the year and a half they had been there, and rejoiced and was quiet when they withdrew.

BURNING OF THE GASPEE

"But," continues Wilson, "quiet could not last long. The flame was sure somewhere to burst out again whenever any incident for a moment stirred excitement. . . . In Rhode Island, in June, 1772, His Majesty's armed schooner *Gaspee* was taken by assault and burned, upon a spit of land where she lay aground. It had been her business to watch against infringements of the navigation laws and the vexatious acts of trade; her commander had grown exceptionally insolent in his work; a sloop which he chased had led him on to the spit, where his schooner stuck fast, and the provincials took advantage of her helplessness to burn her. No one could be found who would inform on those who had done the bold thing; the courageous chief justice of the little province flatly denied the right of the English authorities to order the perpetrators to England for trial; and the royal commission which was appointed to look into the whole affair stirred all the Colonies once more to a deep irritation. The far-away House of Burgesses in Virginia very promptly spoke its mind again. It invited the several Colonies to join Virginia in forming committees of correspondence, in order that all might be of one mind and ready for one action against the aggressions of the government in England. The Ministers in London had meantime resolved to pay the provincial judges, at any rate in Massachusetts, out of the English treasury, taxes or no taxes; and the Massachusetts towns had formed committees of correspondence of their own, as Mr. Adams bade."

Chapter II

THE STORM BREAKS

ITHIN less than a year," says Wilson, "from those memorable autumn days of 1773 when the East India Company's ships came into port with their cargoes of tea, the Colonies had set up a Congress at Philadelphia which looked from the first as if it meant to do things for which there was no law; and which did, in fact, within less than two years after its first assembling, cut the bonds of allegiance which bound America to England. The Colonists did not themselves speak or think of it as a body set up to govern them, or to determine their relations with the government at home, but only as a body organized for consultation and guidance, a general meeting of their committees of correspondence. . . . Mr. Samuel Adams had been deliberately planning revolution in Massachusetts ever since 1768, the year the troops came to Boston to hold the town quiet, while Mr. Townshend's acts strangled its trade; and he had gone the straight way to work to bring it about," by establishing these Colonial committees of correspondence whose members made it their duty to force men to express their opinions; to provoke discussion; to compel people to declare themselves or else seem indifferent; most of all, to see to it "that Mr. Samuel Adams's opinions were duly promulgated and established by argument."

[200]

From *Harper's Magazine*, July, 1896

CARPENTER'S HALL, PHILADELPHIA, WHERE THE FIRST AND SECOND CONTINENTAL
CONGRESSES HELD THEIR SESSIONS

Virginia in particular was quick to take action in support of Massachusetts when she learned of the passage of the Coercive Act which suspended the Massachusetts charter and closed the port of Boston. Indeed, in May, 1774, a month before the text itself of the act had reached the Colonies, the Virginia House of Burgesses ordered "that June 1st, the day the Boston Port bill was to go into effect, be set apart as a day of fasting and prayer—a prayer that civil war might be averted and that the people of America might be united in a common cause."

The governor of Virginia forthwith dissolved the assembly for this act of rebellion, but the members adjourned to the Raleigh tavern, where action was taken toward issuing a call for a congress of all the Colonies. Ever since the *Gaspee* affair, the radical leaders, among them Patrick Henry, Richard Henry Lee, and Thomas

Jefferson, had been meeting quietly of evenings in a private room of this old tavern to decide the action which Virginia now resolved to take, and which resulted in the gathering at Philadelphia in September of that year of the notable men who formed the first Continental Congress.

"On the 9th of September, 1774, four days after the assembling of the Congress at Philadelphia," says Wilson, "delegates from Boston and the other towns in Suffolk County in Massachusetts had met in convention and flatly declared that the acts complained of, being unconstitutional, ought not to be obeyed; that the new judges appointed under the Act of Suspension ought not to be regarded or suffered to act; that the collectors of taxes ought to be advised to retain the moneys collected, rather than turn them into General Gage's treasury; and that, in view of the extraordinary crisis which seemed at hand, the people ought to be counseled to prepare for war—not, indeed, with any purpose of provoking hostilities, but in order, if necessary, to resist aggression. They declared also for a provincial congress, to take the place of the legislative council of their suspended charter, and resolved to

regard the action of the Congress at Philadelphia as law for the common action of the Colonies.

"It gave these resolutions very grave significance that the Congress at Philadelphia unhesitatingly declared, upon their receipt, that the whole continent ought to support Massachusetts in her resistance to the unconstitutional changes in her government, and that any persons who should accept office within the province under the new order of things ought to be considered a public enemy. Moreover, the Suffolk towns did not stand alone. Their temper, it seemed, was the temper

Thomas Jefferson Patrick Henry

R. H. Lee F. L. Lee

In the Old Raleigh Tavern

Illustration from
AT HOME IN VIRGINIA
by Woodrow Wilson

Originally published in
HARPER'S MAGAZINE, *May,* 1896

of the whole Colony. Other towns took action of the same kind; and before the Congress at Philadelphia had adjourned, Massa-

From *Harper's Young People*, May 10, 1889

PAUL REVERE AT LEXINGTON

[204]

chusetts had actually set up a virtually independent provincial congress. General Gage had summoned the regular assembly of the province to meet at Salem, the new capital under the parliamentary changes, on the 5th of October, but had withdrawn the summons as he saw signs of disaffection multiply and his authority dwindle to a mere shadow outside his military lines at Boston. The members of the assembly convened, nevertheless, and, finding no governor to meet them, resolved themselves into a provincial congress and appointed a committee of safety to act as the provisional executive of the Colony. The old government was virtually dissolved, a revolutionary government substituted."

THE BATTLE OF LEXINGTON

After the adjournment of the provincial congress, it became known to General Gage that among the Revolutionary leaders who had gone to Lexington for a few days of rest were John Hancock and Samuel Adams, orders for whose arrest and trial in England he had received some months before. He also knew that the military supplies which the provincials had been gathering were stored at Concord and that patriot companies were being drilled nightly throughout the Colonies. Deciding, therefore, to kill two birds with one stone—arrest Hancock and Adams at Lexington and then seize the arms and ammunition stored at Concord, on the night of the 18th of April, 1775, Gage secretly plotted to send a force of eight hundred regulars to Lexington and Concord. But the patriot leaders discovered his plans, and on that same moonlight night, far in advance of the British, Paul Revere, with two companions, galloped along the country roads, warning all of the approach of the regulars. As the British advanced, the alarm bells and signal guns that they heard warned them of their own danger, and the British commander very prudently sent to Boston for reinforcements. When the regulars reached Lexington Green, just after sunrise on the morning of April 19th, they found themselves confronted by thirty-eight minute men under Captain Parker, who said to his men, "Don't fire unless you are fired upon; but if they want war, it may as well

14

begin here." And, as Higginson, says, "it began there; they were fired upon; they fired rather ineffectually in return, while seven were killed and nine wounded. The rest, after retreating, reformed and pursued the British toward Concord. Then followed the fight at Concord, where four hundred and fifty Americans, instead of thirty-eight, were rallied to meet the British. The fighting took place between two detachments at the North Bridge, where

> "'Once the embattled farmers stood
> And fired the shot heard round the world.'"

The British retreated in disorder, and their return march to Boston ended in a rout, exposed as it was to the guerilla fire of the companies of minute men that sprang up from behind every hedge and clump of trees to take a shot at the retreating foe.

News of the British march on Lexington and Concord and of their disorderly retreat spread rapidly, but hardly more rapidly than the organization of the different bodies of provincial militia which sprang up throughout New England until by the night of the 20th the town of Boston was besieged by an army of sixteen thousand men.

THE BATTLE OF BUNKER HILL

Meanwhile the Second Continental Congress met at Philadelphia on May 10th, and on June 15th appointed Col. George Washington of Virginia commander-in-chief of the troops investing Boston that had now become the national army. Two days later five thousand British soldiers attempted to take by assault Bunker Hill, whose heights the Americans had

Patrick Henry   Washington   Edmund Pendleton

Leaving Mount Vernon for the Congress of the Colonies

Illustration from
AT HOME IN VIRGINIA
by Woodrow Wilson

Originally published in
HARPER'S MAGAZINE, *May*, 1896

fortified. The British attack was twice beaten back, the Colonials retiring upon the third assault only because their powder had given out. The Americans were beaten, but the British had won the hill

From *Harper's Magazine*, October, 1883

LEXINGTON GREEN—"IF THEY WANT WAR, IT MAY AS WELL BEGIN HERE"

Watching the Fight at Bunker Hill

Illustration from
COLONIES AND NATION
by Woodrow Wilson

Originally published in
HARPER'S MAGAZINE, *October*, 1901

at the cost of fifteen hundred men compared with an American loss of only four hundred—truly reason enough for the monument which was built there in honor of these raw recruits that withstood for two hours the attack of the British veterans.

At this point it is important to relate a most dramatic incident that occurred in December, 1774—four months before the battle of Lexington and six months before Bunker Hill, which, in fact, led

From *Harper's Magazine*, July, 1886
BRINGING THE POWDER TO BUNKER HILL

to the British attack at Lexington and saved the Americans from a disastrous defeat at Bunker Hill.

According to Ballard Smith's article in *Harper's Magazine*, July, 1886, this little-known incident in the Revolutionary War was an attack upon Fort William and Mary in Portsmouth Harbor by a band of young patriots led by John Sullivan, afterward major-general in the Continental Army. He had been sent in 1774 as a delegate from New Hampshire to the first Continental Congress.

Paul Revere Bringing News to Sullivan

Illustration from
THE GUNPOWDER FOR BUNKER HILL
by Ballard Smith

Originally published in
HARPER'S MAGAZINE, *July,* 1886

Upon his return in September he felt that the appeal to arms could not much longer be delayed.

"On the afternoon of December 13th Paul Revere (the same who escaped the vigilance of Howe's guards four months later and spread the news along the road from Boston to Lexington of Pitcairn's intended march) rode up to Sullivan's house in Durham." Revere was the bearer of a message from the Massachusetts Committee of Safety that "the king in council had prohibited the importation of arms or military stores into the Colonies," and that preparations were being made to send two regiments to occupy Portsmouth and the fort in its harbor. To Sullivan this meant that immediate action must be taken. In the fort there was a large supply of powder and a quantity of small arms which must be obtained for employment in the patriot cause. Recruiting a small force of patriots whom he had been drilling now for some months, he told them his plans. What followed is briefly told by Eleazer Bennett, a member of the heroic band: "We took a gondola . . . and went down the river to Portsmouth. It was a clear, cold, moonlight night. We sailed down to the fort at the mouth of Piscataqua Harbor. The water was so shallow that we could not bring the boat to within a rod of shore. We waded through the water in perfect silence, mounted the fort, surprised the garrison, and bound the captain. In the fort we found one hundred casks of powder and one

The Fort-Hillers

hundred small arms. In wading through the water it froze upon us."
The powder and small arms were brought to Durham, where they

From *Harper's Magazine*, July, 1886
SURRENDER OF FORT WILLIAM AND MARY

were buried under the pulpit of the meeting house from which Parson
Adams had for years back been inculcating lessons of patriotism.

This captured powder six months later saved the day at Bunker Hill. Colonel Prescott, who had occupied Breed's Hill, finding that he had barely one round of ammunition left, was obliged to give the order to retreat. Both his and the New Hampshire men under Stark, who had hastened to Prescott's succor, would, says Bancroft, "undoubtedly have been cut to pieces or captured except for the galling fire with which Stark, from behind the grass-stuffed fence on Bunker Hill, met the Welsh Fusiliers who were marching

From *Harper's Magazine*, July, 1896

LADY WASHINGTON'S ARRIVAL AT HEADQUARTERS, CAMBRIDGE

to cut off the retreat to Cambridge." The needful powder had reached Stark in the nick of time. "It had been brought," as Ballard Smith relates, "over from Durham, sixty miles away, in old John Demerett's oxcart, and it was a part of the store that had been buried under Parson Adams's pulpit. Failing it, Prescott might on that day have shared the martyrdom of Warren, and Molly Stark might indeed have been a widow that night."

The Storm Breaks

When Washington reached Cambridge on July 3, 1775, to assume direction of the military operations, among the many serious problems that confronted him was this same lack of ammunition. For weeks at a time there was not powder enough to furnish half a pound to a man, exclusive of what the soldiers had in their pouches. Should this become known by the troops before fresh supplies arrived, Washington feared the army would be ruined. There is no evidence to show that the New Hampshire committee sent more powder to the army, but, as all the powder captured at Fort William and Mary was not sent to Bunker Hill, it is possible that Sullivan's daring assault of the previous December again served the American troops in good stead.

What with the general lack of all the things an army needed and the fact that the army was composed of men who had been enlisted for only a few months' service, it was indeed fortunate for Washington that the inactivity of the British gave him all that winter to get his army into fighting trim.

MRS. WASHINGTON'S ARRIVAL IN CAMBRIDGE

"The monotony of the long, anxious season," writes Woodrow Wilson in his life of *George Washington*, "was broken at Cambridge by a touch now and again of such pleasures as spoke of home and gracious peace. In midwinter Mrs. Washington was driven into camp, come all the way from Virginia, with a proper escort, in her coach and four, her horses bestridden by black postilions in their livery of scarlet and white; and she had seemed to bring with her to the homely place not only the ceremonious habit, but the genial and hospitable air of Virginia as well."

By the coming of spring the siege cannon, the powder, and the other needful supplies that had come during the winter months enabled Washington to assume the offensive. Under cover of night Washington had safely gotten a strong force intrenched on Dorchester Heights, and when the sun rose on the morning of March 5, 1776, the British were as startled to see the Americans there as they had been a year before to see them on Bunker Hill. Realizing that Boston was no longer tenable, the British now made hasty preparations to depart, and evacuated the town on March 17th, leaving to Washington stores and military supplies of all kinds.

SERGEANT JASPER AT THE BATTLE OF FORT MOULTRIE, JUNE 28, 1776.

Thus the year 1776 was a memorable one in Revolutionary annals, marked as it was by many dramatic events, among them Washington's unfurling over the Continental Army of the first Union flag of thirteen stripes. This well-remembered event occurred at Cambridge, Massachusetts, on January 1, 1776. On that same day the city of Norfolk, Virginia, was burned by the fleet of Governor Dunmore, whom the people of Virginia, infuriated by his declaration of martial law and his attempt to make Norfolk the rendezvous for a British fleet, had driven to sea. The part of the city escaping Dunmore's cannonading was presently burned by the Virginians themselves to prevent it from becoming a shelter to the enemy. Disappointment, however, had come to the American forces when the advance into Canada under Montgomery and Arnold was repulsed at Quebec, December 30, 1775, necessitating as it did the retirement, June 18, 1776, of the army under Generals Thomas and Sullivan to Crown Point. "But in the Carolinas, about the same time," writes Higginson, "it was the British who were disappointed, and the defense of Fort Moultrie especially gave comfort to all the patriotic party. It was a brilliant achievement, when the fate of Charleston and the Carolinas was determined

Sergeant Jasper at the Battle of Fort Moultrie

Illustration from
THE DAWNING OF INDEPENDENCE
by Thomas Wentworth Higginson

Originally published in
HARPER'S MAGAZINE, *October,* 1883

by the defense of a fortress of palmetto logs, manned by less than five hundred men, under Moultrie, aided by Motte, Marion, and the since renowned Sergeant Jasper. They had thirty-one cannon, but only a scanty supply of powder. Over them waved the flag of blue with a crescent inscribed, 'Liberty.' Against them was a squadron of British ships, some of them carrying fifty guns; and they defended themselves so successfully for ten hours that the British invasion was checked and then abandoned."

During the bombardment by the English fleet the South Carolina flag was shot from its flagstaff and fell outside the fort, whereupon Sergeant Jasper, a youth who could not read or write, leaped down from one of the embrasures, seized the fallen banner, and, having fixed the colors to a sponge staff, stuck the improvised flagstaff in the sand on one of the bastions, and then returned to his place in the fort. This act of heroism at Fort Moultrie compares with any displayed at Bunker Hill the year previous, or, indeed, with that of any engagement anywhere during the war, in which there were so many examples of the heroic valor of men who were fighting for their freedom.

Chapter III

THE COLONIES DECLARE THEIR INDEPENDENCE

AFTER evacuating Boston the British withdrew to Halifax, thus leaving no army in America. But it was not to be for long, and, as Washington had foreseen when he prepared for the defense of New York, the next move of the British was to capture New York, whose strategic position at the mouth of the Hudson would give its possessor control of the heart of the country. And sure enough, on June 28th—the very day of the heroic defense of Fort Moultrie, which had given pause to the British attack on Charleston—a British squadron appeared in New York Bay prepared to land thirty thousand troops from their transports.

Only the month before the Continental Congress had met for its third session, and by this time the spirit of independence had increased to its full growth in all the Colonies. North Carolina had already instructed her delegates sent to the Congress to unite in a declaration of independence. On June 7th Richard Henry Lee, in obedience to instructions from Virginia, offered the resolution "that these United Colonies are, and of right ought to be, free and independent states, and that they are absolved from all allegiance to the British Crown." By the end of June every Colony except

New York had voted in favor of the resolution. A committee, of which Thomas Jefferson was chairman, was then elected to put the resolution in the form in which the world knows it; and on July 4, 1776, the Declaration of Independence as written by Thomas Jefferson was adopted by all the Colonies except New York. New York, however, gave it her sanction five days later, thus making its adoption unanimous.

THE FIRST READING OF THE DECLARATION OF INDEPENDENCE

"On the 8th of July, 1776, at Philadelphia," quoting from an article in *Harper's Weekly*, July 10, 1880, "a procession of intelligent

From *Harper's Magazine*, July, 1892

AT BOSTON, MASSACHUSETTS

Americans passed out of the venerable State House and, ascending a platform at the front on Walnut Street, prepared to commit an act of treason against King George, of daring self-devotion to the interests of mankind. They had not only declared themselves free, independent; they were resolved to read publicly their declaration to their countrymen and the world. It was to be the signal to the people to rise from their bondage in Europe and America. We who

The First Public Reading of the Declaration of
Independence

Illustration from
THE FIRST PUBLIC READING OF THE DECLARATION
OF INDEPENDENCE
by Eugene Lawrence

Originally published in
HARPER'S WEEKLY, *July 10,* 1880

can survey the political and moral progress of a hundred years—since Franklin, Adams, Jefferson, and their associates proclaimed themselves rebels at Philadelphia—may distinctly trace the wonderful results of their rare courage, their greatness. To them the future was covered with doubt and gloom. Yet it is seldom that men who do great deeds are wholly without a consciousness of the good that must follow from them. The calm Franklin felt that the New World was prepared for freedom; the ardent Adams glowed with the thought that future generations would celebrate the day with bonfires and glad congratulations. They could only faintly see as yet the beginning of a new era; perhaps it might early close

From *Harper's Magazine*, July, 1892

AT CHARLESTON, SOUTH CAROLINA

in disaster and public ruin. The war was already upon them. The immense military power of England was directed against the Colonies. The vast fleets of Howe and the great army of invasion had gathered in New York Harbor. All the powers of reaction were in league to crush the voice of struggling truth, and the declaration of human rights so boldly published at Philadelphia might soon be trodden under foot by the mercenary soldiers of the king.

"The day was fine, the sun shone brightly. An immense throng of people had gathered around the State House to listen to the language of freedom. All was joy and hope. There was no trace of fear in all the great multitude, but an assurance of final triumph. At twelve o'clock the city officials, the Congressmen, the sheriff, and the reader were at their posts. John Nixon, who

[222]

In the Reading Room of a New York Coffee House

Illustration from
OLD NEW YORK TAVERNS
by John Austin Stevens

Originally published in
HARPER'S MAGAZINE, *May,* 1890

had been selected on account of his sonorous voice to read for the first time the Declaration to the people, led the procession of the representatives as they filed from their chamber to the public rostrum. Franklin came next, almost the founder of the new nation. He was now seventy years old, his frame still vigorous, his intellect, like Plato's, growing calmer and clearer with time. The next ten years of his life were to be the most laborious and the most important of all. He had snatched the lightning from the heavens; he was

From *Harper's Magazine*, July, 1892

IN NEW YORK (AT HEADQUARTERS)

now to wrest the scepter from the hands of tyrants. Franklin's venerable face and form on this memorable occasion, as he modestly walked to the platform, must have convinced the people that philosophy and discretion were now satisfied that there was no hope for freedom but in resistance. He had pledged his liberty and life for his country. Next came the impulsive orator, John Adams, to whose effective eloquence on the 2d of July is ascribed the final passage of the act of independence. He was thirty years younger than Franklin, in the full strength of his powers. Eager, ardent, ambitious, studious, the cultivated schoolmaster of Worcester had now become one of the world's benefactors. Beside him, and still younger—he was only thirty-three—the tall, thin form of Thomas Jefferson might be seen, the author of the admirable appeal. The keenest, subtlest intellect of his time, Jefferson had embraced the principles of democracy with ardor, and labored to discover and heal the woes of the people. Samuel Adams followed, the pure democrat, who believed more than Jefferson taught, whose life of self-devotion proved the value of freedom. To him John Adams was accustomed to ascribe the decisive blow that divided the New World from the Old. He determined the future fate of generations

From *Harper's Magazine*, July, 1892

AT WILLIAMSBURG, VIRGINIA

of men. Hancock was with them, the polished, graceful merchant, wealthy, singularly aspiring, who bore Washington's rise to the chief command of the army with some impatience, but whose courageous hand signed, as President of Congress, the first copy of the Declaration alone.

"Then Charles Carroll appeared, who afterward, at the signing, when some one said there were several of his name, fixed upon himself the glory and danger of the act, and wrote, 'of Carrollton.' Hopkinson, comic poet and political writer; Robert Morris, the financier whose loans and credit saved the army in its moment of extreme destitution; McKean, the learned delegate from Delaware; Samuel Chase, the worthy associate of Carroll, from Maryland;

and Edward Rutledge, the brilliant patriot from South Carolina—complete our picture. These were a few only of that rare, memorable body of men who signed the Declaration. They were of varied qualities, of almost equal excellence. Jefferson, austere and philosophic, represented the extreme school of the thought of the day—he embodied it in his famous composition; Charles Carroll, cultivated in all the graces of Parisian society, a Roman Catholic, educated in France; the polished Hancock; Rutledge; Chase—threw over the assembly something of the formal manner of the

From *Harper's Magazine*, July, 1892

AT NEWPORT, RHODE ISLAND

ancient regime. The stern severity of Samuel Adams showed what republicanism must be. Wiser and truer men never lived than these representatives of America. But as yet the traitor's doom hung over them; the executioners were assembled in New York Bay.

"Meditative and composed, they showed no fear. It is said that Nixon's sonorous voice filled all the great assembly, that it was heard distinctly on the opposite side of the street, that not an accent faltered nor a word was lost. For the first time the remarkable paper, that for more than a hundred years has been sounding

Reading the Declaration Before Washington's
Army, New York, July 9, 1776

Illustration from
HOW THE DECLARATION WAS RECEIVED
IN THE OLD THIRTEEN
By Charles D. Deshler

Originally published in
HARPER'S MAGAZINE, *July,* 1892

in the ears of men, was declaimed at Philadelphia; it had all the attractions of novelty, all the force of deep conviction. Happy the men who heard for the first time its germ of wisdom! Happy those who could so hail its perilous truths! 'We believe,' exclaimed the first confessors and martyrs, 'that all men are born free and equal; we believe in our indestructible rights; we proclaim ourselves independent.' It is easy to imagine the intense interest of the people, the unbounded joy, the sense of a new existence. They cheered, they shouted. For the rest of the day Philadelphia was given up to enthusiastic rejoicings. The people wandered cheering through the streets; at night bonfires and illuminations lit up the scene. The reading of the Declaration awoke everywhere the same enthusiastic ardor. At Princeton, the college glowed at night with a fine illumination.

From *Harper's Magazine*, July, 1892

AT PORTSMOUTH, NEW HAMPSHIRE

THE DECLARATION IS READ TO THE ARMY IN NEW YORK

"Washington, at New York, July 9th, while the guns of the English armada were heard at the Narrows, ordered the Declaration to be read before the army. It was received with shouts of joy. That night the patriots tore down the gilded statue of King George in the Bowling Green, and soon after cast it into bullets. The Eastern towns surpassed the zeal of Philadelphia and New York. Boston, just snatched from the grasp of the tyrant, broke into fierce enthusiasm. The Declaration was read, July 17th, in Faneuil Hall; the city was filled with a rejoicing multitude; speeches, cheers, congratulations, bonfires, music, lights, filled all the day and night; new hope descended upon man, the prospect of a better life. . . .

The Colonies Declare Their Independence

"The Declaration was not commented upon in the newspapers of the day. They were content with printing it. Said the Philadelphia *Post*, July 9th, 'Yesterday, at twelve o'clock, INDEPENDENCY was declared at the State House in this city, in the presence of many thousand spectators, who testified their approbation of it by repeated acclamations of joy.' In the same paper a negro child is advertised for sale, and several slaves. On another page is an account of the English fleet that is gathering in New York Harbor, and a letter from the West Indies that tells the provincials there is no hope of

From *Harper's Magazine*, July, 1892

AT PHILADELPHIA, PENNSYLVANIA

pardon for them but in submission. In the next issue the fleet from Halifax is described as forming a line in New York Bay from the Kill von Kull to Simonson's Ferry, on the east side of Staten Island. The *Asia* had already fired her guns into the houses on Long Island, in reply to a small battery on the shore. It is sometimes said that the Declaration was of little importance, that it was forgotten in the strife of arms. But this is an error. The Declaration was the decision, the public avowal, the consensus that joined America and freedom. The tie could never be broken. Howe came too late with his offers of grace and pardon. The decision was made; America was free. The reading of the Declaration of Independence on the 8th of July, 1776, was the decisive act that published to mankind the opening of a new era; before it the fleets and armies of England were powerless, and Europe and America rose into new life together."

The two months immediately following, however, were to see the darkest days of the Revolution. The British force put ashore at New York in August outnumbered the American army two to one, and Washington was forced to retire from Brooklyn Heights and Long Island to the heights overlooking the Harlem River, where he held out until November.

THE HEROISM OF NATHAN HALE

While there Washington sent out a call for a man who would be willing to enter the British lines and bring back information as to the strength and probable plans of the enemy. Such a man he found in Capt. Nathan Hale, a graduate of Yale and one of those who had taken part in the siege of Boston. Hale, volunteering to attempt the dangerous task, entered the British camp on Long Island, disguised, some accounts say, as a plain young farmer, others as a school-teacher, and made sketches and notes unsuspected. His task accomplished, he was about to take the ferry to Brooklyn, when a Tory who had recognized him the night before in a tavern betrayed him. He was taken to Howe's headquarters at the Beekman mansion and confined in the greenhouse all night. He frankly avowed his name, rank, and character as a spy, and, without even the form of a trial, was handed over to the cruel provost marshal, Cunningham, the next morning to be hanged. That infamous officer denied Hale the services of a clergyman and the use of a bible; but the more humane officer who superintended the execution furnished him with materials to write letters to his mother, his betrothed, and sisters. These the brutal Cunningham destroyed before the face of his victim, while tears and sobs marked the sympathy of the spectators. With unfaltering voice Hale said, at the last moment, "I only regret that I have but one life to lose for my country." A statue, erected in honor of Hale's patriotism, now stands in City Hall Park, New York City.

Thus the young captain died the death of a hero, while Washington, without the information Hale had given his life to secure, continued to hold his position along the Hudson through September, October, and part of November. Determined to gain the rear of the American army and thus cut off Washington's retreat to the north, on the 17th of November, General Howe with the larger part of his army stormed Fort Washington. This fort, with Fort Lee on the

From *Harper's Magazine*, June, 1880

HALE RECEIVING INSTRUCTIONS FROM WASHINGTON

opposite shore, had barred his way to the possession of the Hudson, so necessary to the British plan to control the heart of the country. After a stubborn resistance Fort Washington was compelled to surrender its garrison of three thousand men with its great stock of artillery and small arms. After such a disaster, Washington was forced to abandon the Hudson and begin his famous retreat across New Jersey.

"Yet," as Higginson says, "amid all these accumulated disasters Washington wrote to Congress that he could see 'without despondency even for a moment' what America called her 'gloomy hours.' He could breathe more freely at last when, on December 8th, he crossed the Delaware at Trenton with what the discouraged Reed had called 'the wretched fragments of a broken army,' now diminished to three thousand men. As his last boat crossed, the

From *Harper's Magazine*, June, 1880
"I ONLY REGRET THAT I HAVE BUT ONE LIFE TO LOSE FOR MY COUNTRY"

advanced guard of Howe's army reached the river and looked eagerly for means of transportation. Washington had seized everything that could float upon the water within seventy miles. . . .

"He surprised the Hessians at Trenton, recrossing the river and returning on his course with what was perhaps the most brilliant single stroke of war that he ever achieved. A few days later (January 3, 1777) he defeated Cornwallis at Princeton with almost

Carnival at Philadelphia

Illustration from
THE BATTLE OF MONMOUTH COURT-HOUSE
by Benson J. Lossing

Originally published in
HARPER'S MAGAZINE, *June,* 1878

equal ability; and all this he did with but five thousand men, one half militia, the rest little more. . . . The dawn of independence seemed overcast indeed when the campaign of 1776 closed, and Washington, with only three or four thousand men, went sadly into winter quarters at Morristown.

" . . . The year that followed, however, was in many respects the turning point of the Revolution. The British had formed a

From *Harper's Magazine*, January, 1881

THE BRITISH IN WILMINGTON AFTER THE BATTLE OF BRANDYWINE

plan which, had it been carried out, might have resulted in a complete triumph for them. It was a project to take thorough possession of the whole line of the Hudson—Burgoyne coming down from the north, Howe going up from the south—thus absolutely cutting the Colonies in two, separating New England from the rest, and conquering each by itself. Happily this was abandoned for a measure that had no valuable results, the possession of Philadelphia. It is true that in the effort to save that city, Washington sustained defeat at Brandywine (September 11, 1777), and only came near victory, without achieving it, at Germantown (October 4th). But the occupation of Philadelphia divided the British army—now nearly fifty thousand soldiers—while the American army, though it had shrunk to about half that number, remained more concentrated. Moreover, the luxurious winter in Philadelphia did the invading troops little good"; the soldiers with their loyalist friends making it a season of gayety—with all kinds of revelry, ending in a wild carnival; "while the terrible winter at Valley Forge was in one sense the saving of the Americans. There they came under

From *Harper's Magazine*, October, 1889

THE WOUNDED SOLDIERS SAT ALONG THE WALL

After the bloody Battle of Brandywine in 1777 nearly three hundred American soldiers were brought to the Dunker Sisters' House at Ephrata, near Lancaster, Pennsylvania. There they were kindly nursed by the devout sisters of the Dunker or German Baptist sect who called themselves "God's Peculiar People."

the influence of trained foreign officers—Pulaski and Steuben, as well as the young Lafayette. Baron Steuben especially took the hungry soldiers and taught them what drill meant.

"Meanwhile," Higginson continues, "at the north there occurred successes for the American army which grew directly out of the abandonment of the British plan. Stark with New

England troops defeated a detachment of Burgoyne's army near Bennington; and Gates took the whole of that army—five thousand men—prisoners at Saratoga, October 17, 1777. It seemed for the moment that this determined the fate of the war. . . . But the surrender of Burgoyne at least turned the scale in favor of the Americans, so far as the judgment of Europe was

From *Harper's Magazine*, January, 1881

THE DESTRUCTION OF THE SIGN

When the British occupied Wilmington in 1777 two sailors, dressed in petticoat trousers, taking offense at an inn sign commemorating the victory of an American sloop over two British three-deckers, pulled it down and hacked it to pieces.

[236]

Washington and Steuben at Valley Forge

Illustration from
GENERAL WASHINGTON
by Woodrow Wilson

Originally published in
HARPER'S MAGAZINE, *July,* 1896

concerned." As a result of this victory the king of France recognized the independence of the United States in December of that year, and on February 8th of the following year was signed the treaty of alliance by which the United States agreed with France not to make peace with England until that country should acknowledge her independence.

Two results immediately flowed from the French alliance —one, the declaration of war by England against France, and the withdrawal of the British army from Philadelphia. Sir Henry Clinton had been assigned to the chief command in place of the easy-going, voluptuous

From *Harper's Magazine*, April, 1880
WASHINGTON'S HEADQUARTERS, VALLEY FORGE

Howe, and, fearing the approach of the French fleet, he at once proceeded with his army to New York, across New Jersey. Having occupied Philadelphia with American troops, Washington was soon at the heels of Clinton's army, overtaking him near Monmouth,

[238]

New Jersey, upon the morning of June 28th. There occurred the first clash between the enemy and the American forces in command of Gen. Charles Lee, a renegade Englishman, whose disgraceful conduct on that day branded him as a traitor to the patriot cause. To Lee had been assigned the task of attacking the British in flank and checking their advance until the main army under Washington should arrive. Generals Wayne and Lafayette had already advanced to the attack, when Lee's orders halted them. Then all became confusion, and when Washington came up at full gallop he met the disordered troops, with Lee in the van, beating a precipitate retreat. Washington had reached the front

From *Harper's Magazine*, April, 1880

WASHINGTON'S PRIVATE OFFICE, VALLEY FORGE

in the nick of time. According to Lafayette, "His Excellency's face was terrible" as he demanded from Lee an explanation of his conduct. With Washington himself now in command, the retreat was soon changed to an attack, and while it was still night Clinton and his army marched "by the light of the moon" to their boats off Sandy Hook, leaving the Americans in possession of the field.

[239]

Monmouth, the last general engagement in the north, but for the treachery of Charles Lee, might well have been the greatest battle of the Revolution. Both armies were nearly equal in numbers; and on the American side nearly all the officers who won fame in the Revolutionary struggle took part in the fighting. Among them were Nathaniel Greene of Rhode Island, probably Washing-

From *Harper's Magazine*, December, 1879

A REVOLUTIONARY RECRUITING OFFICE—PRIVATEERSMEN IN NEW LONDON

ton's greatest general, and Anthony Wayne of Pennsylvania, the most daring of all the American commanders, who a year later captured the British fortifications at Stony Point, on the Hudson; Lafayette; Alexander Hamilton; and Aaron Burr, who twenty-six years later killed Hamilton in a duel fought under the rocky cliffs of Weehawken, New Jersey.

AMERICAN PRIVATEERS

Meanwhile, the hardy seafaring men, especially of New York and New England, had quickly taken to privateering as soon as

Fight Between "Bonhomme Richard" and
"Serapis"

Illustration from
COLONIES AND NATION
by Woodrow Wilson

Originally published in
HARPER'S MAGAZINE, *October*, 1901

Congress in 1776 permitted Americans to fit out armed vessels to prey on British commerce. Before the French alliance gave America a navy with which to dispute England's sea power, this was the only

From *Harper's Magazine*, January, 1884

THE FRENCH OFFICERS AT NEWPORT

means the young republic had of interfering with the British ships that were bringing supplies to British armies in America. Commerce destroying was the chief aim of these American privateers,

An American Privateer Taking a British Prize

Illustration from
PENNSYLVANIA'S DEFIANCE OF THE UNITED STATES
by Hampton L. Carson

Originally published in
HARPER'S MAGAZINE, *October,* 1908

and in the cruising warfare which their ships carried on they not only did tremendous damage to the British West India trade, but also brought many valuable British prizes to port.

Quoting again from Higginson: "The direct service done by the French alliance was of less value than the moral support it brought. It occupied Newport, Rhode Island, in July, 1780, with nearly six thousand men in army and navy. The unpublished memorials of that time and place contain many delightful recollections of the charming manners of the French officers; of the Rochambeaux, father and son; of the Duc de Deux-Ponts, afterward king of Bavaria; of the Prince de Broglie, guillotined in the Revolution; of the Swedish Count Fersen, 'the Adonis of the camp,' who afterward acted as coachman for the French king and queen in their escape from Paris; of the Vicomte de Noailles and of Admiral de Ternay, the latter buried in Trinity Churchyard in Newport. There are old houses in that city which still retain upon their windowpanes the gallant inscriptions of those picturesque days, and there are old letters and manuscripts that portray their glories. One that lies before me describes the young noblemen driving into the country upon parties of pleasure, preceded by their running footmen—a survival of feudalism—tall youths in kid slippers and with leaping poles; another describes the reception of Washington by the whole French garrison, in March, 1781. It was a brilliant scene. The four French regiments were known as Bourbonnais, Soissonnais, Deux-Ponts, and Saintonge; they contained each a thousand men; and the cavalry troop, under De Lauzun, was almost as large. Some of these wore white uniforms, with yellow or violet or crimson lapels, and with black gaiters; others had a uniform of black and gold, with gaiters of snowy white. The officers displayed stars and badges; even the officers' servants were gay in gold and silver lace. Over them all and over the whole town floated the white flag of the Bourbons with the fleurs-de-lis. They were drawn up in open ranks along the avenue leading to the long wharf, which was just then losing its picturesque old name, Queen's Hithe. This gay army, whose fresh uniforms and appointments contrasted strangely with the worn and dilapidated aspect of the Continental troops, received Washington with the honors due to a marshal of France.

From *Harper's Magazine*, November, 1901

WASHINGTON AND ROCHAMBEAU IN THE TRENCHES AT YORKTOWN

[244]

"In the evening a ball was given to the American generals. Washington opened the dance with the beautiful Miss Champlin; he chose for the figure the country dance known as 'A Successful Campaign,' and, as he danced, the French officers took the instruments from the musicians and themselves played the air and accompaniment. Thus with characteristic graces began

The Surrender of Cornwallis at Yorktown

Illustration from
THE SURRENDER OF CORNWALLIS
Originally published in
HARPER'S WEEKLY, *October 22, 1881*

the French occupation of Newport, and it continued to be for them rather a holiday campaign until the siege of Yorktown, Virginia, proved the qualities of their engineers and their soldiers; and in the great painting which represents the scene, at the Versailles palace, General de Rochambeau is made the conspicuous figure, while Washington is quite secondary.

FIGHT BETWEEN "BONHOMME RICHARD" AND THE "SERAPIS"

"Meanwhile," continues Higginson, "the successes of Paul Jones in sea fighting gained still more the respect of Europe, and his victorious fight of three hours in the *Bonhomme Richard* against the *Serapis* (1779)—the two ships being lashed side to side—was the earliest naval victory gained under the present American flag, which this bold sea captain was the first to unfurl. Then the skillful campaigns of Gen. Nathaniel Greene (1780) rescued the Carolinas from invasion; and the treason of Benedict Arnold, with his plan for surrendering to the British the 'American Gibraltar'—West Point—created a public excitement only deepened by the melancholy death of Major André, who was hanged as a spy, September 23, 1780." It was André's letter to Arnold, telling him of his detention, that warned the latter of his own danger, and gave him ample time to escape in the British sloop-of-war *Vulture*.

SURRENDER OF CORNWALLIS AT YORKTOWN

In August of the following year, the Count de Graase arrived off the Virginia coast with a powerful French fleet, and Washington, taking advantage of this good fortune, suddenly moved his army from the Hudson to the James and invested Yorktown with an overwhelming force. Finding his escape impossible, Cornwallis now asked Washington for terms, and, these being agreed to, he himself and his army of some seven thousand men became prisoners of war.

Thus, October 19, 1781, was brought to a victorious close the war of the American Revolution. No sooner had Cornwallis laid down his arms than Washington chose Colonel Tilghman, his aid-de-camp, to bear the great news to Congress, then in session in

The Escape of Arnold on the British Sloop-of-War
"Vulture"

Illustration from
GENERAL WASHINGTON
by Woodrow Wilson

Originally published in
HARPER'S MAGAZINE, *July,* 1896

Philadelphia, and great was the rejoicing by the people, to whom the messenger told the glad tidings as he rode from Yorktown to Philadelphia.

"For nearly two years after the surrender of Cornwallis the British troops," says Higginson, "held the cities of New York, Charleston, and Savannah; and though they were powerless beyond those cities, yet it seemed to their garrisons, no doubt, that the war was not yet ended. . . .

"Independence was essentially secured by the preliminary articles signed in Paris on January 20, 1783, although the final treaty was not signed till September 3d. It was on April 18, 1783, that Washington issued his order for the cessation of hostilities, thus completing, as he said, the eighth year of the war."

WASHINGTON REFUSES A DICTATORSHIP

With returning peace, the prospects of the Continental Army, about to be mustered out, appeared very gloomy. Throughout the winter of 1782–83 the conditions in the country were such that many feared a renewal of the war. It was necessary, therefore, still to maintain the army, the main body of which was assembled at Newburg on the Hudson, where Washington had his headquarters. For a long time neither officers nor private soldiers had received any pay. Congress had no money, and no certainty as to when it should have any. Discontent was rife in the army and distress was widespread throughout the country. Contemplating the inherent weakness of the new government, many were inclined to consider it a normal condition of the republican form, and wished for a stronger one, like that of Great Britain. This feeling became so manifest in the army that Colonel Nicola, a foreigner by birth, and of weighty character, commanding a Pennsylvania regiment, wrote a reprehensible letter to Washington in May, 1782, in which, professing to speak for the army, he urged the necessity of a monarchy to secure an efficient government and the rights of the people for the Americans. He proposed to Washington to accept the headship of such a government, with the title of king, and assured

He Stops at the Sign of the Weathervane

*Colonel Tilghman on his ride to Philadelphia tells the people on the way
of the American victory at Yorktown*

Illustration from
TILGHMAN'S RIDE FROM YORKTOWN
Originally published in
HARPER'S MAGAZINE, *November*, 1881

him of the support of the army. Nicola received a stern rebuke from this great man, who replied, "If I am not deceived in the knowledge of myself, you could not have found a person to

From *Harper's Magazine*, October, 1883

WASHINGTON REFUSING A DICTATORSHIP

whom your schemes are more disagreeable." Thus the great Washington crushed in its bud the conspiracy to overthrow the young republic.

Spending the winter in indolence amid the dreary hills of Newburg and wearily waiting for their wants to be relieved, while the British army was still in New York, sorely tried the patience of these veterans, to whom their country owed so much. Such was

From *Harper's Magazine*, October, 1883

WASHINGTON AND HIS GENERALS IN CONSULTATION, MARCH 15, 1783

the degree of their discontent that in the early part of 1783 the situation became desperate. On March 10th of that year, quoting from McLaughlin in *The Confederation and the Constitution*, "an anonymous paper was circulated suggesting a meeting of the officers of the army for the following day, to consider their grievances and to take steps to bring an end to their sufferings. It was written in language calculated to excite the anger and awaken still further the resentment of the soldiers, who, with much justice, felt that they had sacrificed their comfort and were now treated with scorn and contumely. 'Can you, then, consent to be the only sufferers by this revolution, and, retiring from the field, grow old in poverty, wretchedness, and contempt? Can you consent to wade through the vile mire of dependency and owe the miserable remnant of that life to charity, which has hitherto been spent in honor?— If you can—go—and carry with you the jest of Tories and the scorn of Whigs—the ridicule and, what is worse, the pity of the world. Go, starve, and be forgotten! But if your spirit should revolt at this; if you have sense enough to discover, and spirit enough to oppose, tyranny under whatever garb it may assume, whether it be the plain coat of republicanism or the splendid robe of royalty; if you have learned to discriminate between a people and a cause, between men and principles—awake, attend you to your situation, and redress yourselves. If the present moment be lost, every future effort is in vain; and your threats will be as empty as your entreaties now.'"

Whoever wrote this appeal was a master of vehement and forceful English. Knowledge of its circulation reached the ears of Washington, who, sensible of the danger at once, issued a call for his officers to meet him. Washington no doubt feared that in the present desperate state of the army their passions might carry them even to the length of civil war. When his officers were all assembled, Washington appeared, and as he took his place before them drew, says Cobb in the *Writings* of Washington, "his written address from his coat pocket, and his spectacles with the other hand from his waistcoat pocket, and then addressed the officers in the following manner, 'Gentlemen, you will permit me to put on my spectacles, for I have not only grown gray, but almost blind, in the service of my country.' This little address, with the mode and manner of delivering it, drew tears from many of the officers." "And," concluded Washington, "let me conjure you, in the name of our common country, as you value your own sacred honor, as you respect the rights of humanity, and as you regard the military

Mustered Out—A Rest on the Way Home

Illustration from
FIRST IN PEACE
by Woodrow Wilson
Originally published in
HARPER'S MAGAZINE, *September,* 1896

and national character of America, to express your utmost horror and detestation of the man who wishes, under any specious pretenses, to overturn the liberties of our country, and who wickedly

From *Harper's Magazine*, November, 1883

THE LAST BOATLOAD OF THE BRITISH LEAVING NEW YORK

attempts to open the floodgates of civil discord and deluge our rising empire in blood." In reply the officers adopted resolutions express-

[254]

ing approval of Washington's speech and assuring him of their unwavering faith in the justice of Congress and the country; adding that they expected him to see that Congress should give immediate consideration to their claims. The army was finally disbanded November 3, 1783, going home "without a settlement of their accounts or a farthing of money in their pockets."

THE EVACUATION OF NEW YORK BY THE BRITISH

"No part of the country," quoting from *Harper's Weekly*, November 24, 1883, "suffered as did New York from the pains of the Revolution. More than half its territory—and that the most populous and important—lay for seven years in the power of the intruder. It could have neither privateers nor trade. It had no seaboard. Its fine river and harbor were used for its destruction. Of its remaining territory, the larger part was in the very track of the war. The savage inroad of Burgoyne from the north left everywhere traces of desolation. The merciless Clinton covered the shores of the Hudson with the proofs of his barbarity. Towns, villages, and farms he laid in ruins. But even all this might have been borne had not our distracted state been threatened and harried along its borders by the constant invasions of the Indians, and in the interior by the plots and turbulence of the Tories. It is wonderful that Governor Clinton and his almost fugitive legislature were able to maintain its independence, collect their taxes, and contribute so large a share of men, arms, and money to the Continental armies. Clinton, the Livingstons, Willett, Schuyler, McDougal, Varick, Roosevelt, Platt, and, above all, a patient, courageous people, carried New York through seven years of pain and sorrow such as few communities ever bore.

"And now suddenly had come the almost unlooked-for liberation. The invaders, beaten, were about to escape sullenly from the fallen city. It was once more free. For the first time in seven years of captivity Manhattan Island, Staten Island, and Long Island were to hear the notes of their national music and listen to the voice of peace.

THE CONTINENTAL ARMY MARCHES DOWN THE OLD BOWERY, N. Y.,
NOVEMBER 25, 1783

"On the 25th of November, 1783, was performed the last act
of the war of liberation. The people of New York took possession
of their metropolis. For seven years of expectation, doubt, fear, or
exultation Washington had never ceased to keep his eyes fixed
upon the city from which he had fled in 1776, a beaten general.
He had hoped to snatch it away from the foe by some swift strategy
or bold attack. He had won it at last in Virginia, and now was to
enter it in peace. The day, the scene, rise upon us at its hundredth
anniversary. In the morning of the 25th a detachment of the
American army had marched from Harlem as far as Grand Street;
the English troops retired at their approach. The Americans took
possession of the forts, lines, intrenchments, so long held by their
foes. The English and the Tory exiles moved slowly down to the
Battery, and embarked in the great fleet of warships and transports that filled the bay. Reluctant, sad, they passed through the
ruined city, symbols of a dying past, adherents of a political creed
long since banished from among men.

THE CIVIL PROCESSION HEADED BY GENERAL WASHINGTON
AND GOVERNOR CLINTON

"But at the upper end of the island all was exultation and hope.
Escorted by the Westchester Light Guards and followed by a crowd
of citizens and patriot exiles returning joyfully to their homes, two
eminent men rode down together from Harlem to the city. One
was Washington, pale, careworn, exultant, full of hope, and one
Governor George Clinton, active, brave, sincere, the war Governor
of New York. They were both on horseback, of fine appearance
and striking carriage. Both were sincere friends of the people,
possessed of the very spirit of reform. To Clinton New York
owes its common schools and its general education; to Washington
its freedom to follow knowledge. They rode together on that
auspicious day along Bowery Road, down Queen, or what is now
Pearl Street, through Wall to Broadway, amid a crowd of rejoicing

The Continental Army Marching Down the Old
Bowery, New York, November 25, 1783

Illustration from
THE EVACUATION, 1783
by Eugene Lawrence

Originally published in
HARPER'S WEEKLY, *November 24, 1883*

citizens, and saw for the first time in seven years the fair city of their love. But what a change! They came to a city of ruins. How had not New York suffered? It was a picture of despair, lightened only by the new era of hope.

"In the evening there was a memorable dinner at Fraunce's Tavern, on the corner of Broad and Pearl Streets. The room is still shown, almost unchanged, where Washington, Clinton, and the heroes of New York met at this triumphal banquet. Its fare was solid and plain. Toasts were pledged to all who had aided the cause of freedom—the French king, the United Netherlands, the northern powers. With one heart they exclaimed: 'May America be the asylum to the persecuted of the earth!' 'May the remembrance of this day be a lesson to princes!' 'The memory of the heroes who have fallen for our freedom.' All was excitement and hope. A display of fireworks was given a few days later. Of the touching traits of the festal season were the congratulations (November 29th) offered to Washington and Clinton by the exiled patriots, and their replies. 'May the tranquillity of your city be perpetual!' wrote Washington; 'may the ruin be repaired!' 'To your sufferings, and the invincible spirit with which they were surmounted,' wrote Clinton, 'I have been witness.'"

MEETING OF CAPTAIN TOLLEMACHE AND CAPTAIN PENNINGTON AT THE CITY ARMS

Seven days later, on December 2d, at the City Arms Tavern on Broadway, whose walls had echoed so many times to toasts to kings and royal governors, admirals and generals of the crown, a great entertainment, in celebration of peace, was given to General Washington.

"Through all the tramp and bustle of the Revolution," as John Austin Stevens writes in his article, "Old New York Taverns," *Harper's Magazine*, May, 1890, "the City Arms," on the site of which later was built the famous old City Hotel, "continued to hold its own as the chief tavern of the town, though the pretty neighborhood was sadly changed by the terrible fire which swept the

The Civil Procession Headed by General
Washington and Governor Clinton

Illustration from
EVACUATION OF NEW YORK BY THE BRITISH, 1783
by Henry P. Johnson

Originally published in
HARPER'S MAGAZINE, *November*, 1883

city after the entry of the British army in 1776, and its stately neighbor, old Trinity, was burned in the general wreck. Notwithstanding the change, the old locality still maintained sufficient charm to attract such of the fashion of the city as remained during the captivity. The officers of the British army, brilliant in their uniforms, thronged the porch and piazzas, while the girls, who loved the military, paced the Church Walk, as the mall in front of the ruins was called, in the evening promenade. Within were the usual revelry and festivity of a garrison town. On one occasion the old walls were the witness of a terrible tragedy. It was an evening in late September. During the day a fleet of men-of-war, with a heavy convoy of provisions and supplies, had sailed into the harbor. During the voyage a difference had occurred between Hon. J. Tollemache (brother to the Earl of Dysart), the commander of the *Zebra* man-of-war, and Captain Pennington of the Coldstream Guards. The offense was a sonnet written by Captain Pennington, which Captain Tollemache took up as reflecting upon the wit of his lady; suspended at sea by the necessities of the service, the quarrel was renewed on shore. The meeting took place at the tavern. A brace of pistols were first fired without result. When swords were drawn, Captain Tollemache was run through the left breast and instantly expired, while Captain Pennington, who received seven wounds, appears to have survived the encounter. The body of the unfortunate Tollemache lies buried within the grave enclosure of old Trinity."

WASHINGTON TAKES LEAVE OF HIS OFFICERS

On December 4, 1783, Washington assembled his officers, who were near in the large public room of Fraunce's Tavern, to exchange farewells with them. After the officers had assembled, Washington entered the room and, taking a glass of wine in his hand, said: "With a heart full of love and gratitude, I now take leave of you. I most devoutly wish that your latter days may be as prosperous and happy as your former ones have been glorious and honorable." Having tasted the wine, he continued, "I cannot come to each of

Meeting of Captain Tollemache and Captain
Pennington at "The City Arms"

Illustration from
OLD NEW YORK TAVERNS
by John Austin Stevens

Originally published in
HARPER'S MAGAZINE, *May,* 1890

you to take my leave, but shall be obliged to you if each will come and take me by the hand." The scene was touching and impressive. While their cheeks were suffused with tears Washington kissed each of his beloved companions in arms on the forehead. Then the commander-in-chief left the room and, passing through a corps of light infantry, walked to Whitehall Ferry, followed by a vast procession of citizens. At 2 P.M. he entered a barge and crossed the Hudson to Paulus's Hook (now Jersey City), on his way to the Congress at Annapolis.

WASHINGTON BRINGS HIS MOTHER INTO THE BALLROOM

At Annapolis he resigned his commission, and on Christmas Eve he and Mrs. Washington arrived at Mount Vernon, where he was welcomed back to private life by the greetings of his family and a flock of colored servants. Virginia had seen but little of Washington since 1775, when he had left Mount Vernon for the Continental Congress which chose him commander-in-chief of the army. He had, however, stopped at Fredericksburg to visit his mother with Count de Rochambeau, following the victory at Yorktown, before proceeding to the army headquarters at Newburg. There a formal ball was given in celebration of the victory, and before he went north again Washington had the pleasure of entering the ballroom with his aged mother on his arm.

With the year 1783 peace had come, but the murmurs of the discontented were heard everywhere. The states were supreme, while Congress was treated with contempt; unless a respectable government were soon established, the country would soon be in a state of anarchy. Washington realized this and, soon after the army was mustered out, addressed a circular letter to the governors of all the states, urging the necessity of their union under one federal head. All thinking men realized that the Confederation was a failure. Repeated attempts to amend the Articles so as to give more power to Congress had failed, and in the meanwhile Congress grew more and more helpless. Events, however, were soon to take place which would cause the downfall of the Con-

Washington Taking Leave of His Officers,
December 4, 1783

Illustration from
HARPER'S WEEKLY

Originally published
December 4, 1883

federation and the establishment of a stable government. Among such events, the one that startled the conservative men in all the states was the celebrated insurrection of Daniel Shays, which occurred in Massachusetts in the winter of 1786–87.

SHAYS'S REBELLION

At the end of the Revolutionary conflict there was an abundance of specie in circulation in the country, but a great deal of money had to be sent abroad to pay for the European goods with which the American market was flooded as soon as peace had been declared.

In the importation of these foreign goods great recklessness had been displayed, and as a result of the disappearance from circulation of specie, there was a lack of business confidence and a heavy pressure of debt, which gave rise in almost all the states to a great clamor for some quick method of remedying this scarcity of money.

To obtain the needed relief, the great debtor class in the several states demanded the emission of paper money; and in spite of the fact that something could not be created out of nothing merely by having recourse to the printing press, thousands continued to clamor for this method of repudiating their just obligations. Paper money, then, was the panacea for all their ills. "The hoarse laments of the unhappy, who wished for the promised days of plenty and complained that gold and silver had 'taken wings and flown to the other side of the Atlantic,' who demanded that ease and prosperity be brought to each man's door by legislative enactment," says McLaughlin in *Confederation and the Constitution*, was heard throughout all the thirteen states.

As a result of the popular clamor, all the states except New Hampshire, Massachusetts, and Virginia, proceeded to issue paper money in large quantities.

At length in 1786 the situation reached a crisis in Massachusetts, when "a convention of fifty towns" passed a series of resolutions complaining of taxes, courts, lawyers, and scarcity of money, and

Washington Bringing His Mother into the
Ballroom, Fredericksburg

Illustration from
FIRST IN PEACE
by Woodrow Wilson

Originally published in
HARPER'S MAGAZINE, *September,* 1896

asking "to have emitted a bank of paper money, subject to a depreciation as legal tender in payment of all debts—a pleasant plan whereby it was to be arranged that the money should decline by easy stages from par to nothing, in accordance with some predetermined requirements of descent."

This meeting was but the prelude to more radical acts. Armed mobs took possession of courthouses in widely separated sections of the state and prevented the sitting of the court until the grievances of the people should be redressed.

The situation continued to grow worse, becoming nothing short of civil war; rioting was rife in various parts of the state, and so threatening was the crisis that Congress had begun to raise troops, ostensibly to quell the Indians on the frontier, but really to assist Massachusetts if necessary.

"At Springfield," says McLaughlin, "bloodshed was narrowly avoided. The court was protected by the militia; but a mob of one thousand men . . . with arms paraded the streets under the leadership of Daniel Shays, a man . . . who had seen service in the Continental Army and now looked for new fame as the leader of a popular uprising."

A riot occurred for the second time at Worcester, troops had to be sent to put down disturbances at Concord, while the army under Shays that had gathered at Worcester threatened to attack Cambridge, beating a disorderly retreat, however, when steps were taken to protect the city.

"The center of the trouble was now shifted to Springfield, where an army of rebels commanded by Shays, Eli Parsons, and Luke Day was posted." There an attack was made on the arsenal, but on the arrival of troops under General Lincoln, Shays and his forces retreated in great disorder, and Lincoln's forces continued the pursuit until the rebel army had been utterly routed.

Thus the insurrection which for a time seemed to threaten to overwhelm the state government was at length suppressed. "Shays's rebellion merits attention not because it was the only evidence of social disturbance," says McLaughlin, "but because it was the

Shays's Mob in Possession of a Courthouse

Illustration from
THE BIRTH OF A NATION
by Thomas Wentworth Higginson

Originally published in
HARPER'S MAGAZINE, *January*, 1884

conspicuous uprising that startled the thoughtful men of every state and made them wonder what the end of their great war for independence might prove to be." By disclosing the danger of civil war it "helped to bring about a reaction, strengthen the hands of conservatives, discredit extreme democratic tendencies, and aid the men who were seeking to give vigor to the Union. The reaction helped the establishment of new institutions and the creation of a government capable of insuring domestic tranquillity."

Chapter IV

THE NATION FINDS ITSELF

EVEN before Shays's Rebellion in this gloomy year of 1786, five of the thirteen states sent delegates (September, 1786) to a convention held at Annapolis to which they had been invited by James Madison to consider the deplorable business conditions of the Union. This Annapolis convention accomplished but little and is chiefly memorable for having called another convention to meet at Philadelphia in May, 1787; but so strong was the passion for sovereignty in all the states that even Washington did not expect much from it in the way of results. This convention, however, during the summer of 1787, saved the nation by forming the Constitution of the United States, which twelve months later became the law of the land and has remained so ever since.

Thus was created a nation that was neither French nor English, but genuinely American. The Constitution was to go into effect as soon as nine states had ratified it. That having occurred late in June, 1788, Congress appointed the first Wednesday in January, 1789, as the date on which presidential electors should be chosen, and the first Wednesday in February as the date on which the electors should vote for President and Vice-President; also that the new Congress should assemble in New York on the first Wednesday in March. Thus the Continental Congress went out of existence on March 4, 1789.

As the choice for President no one was thought of but Washington—the idol of all the states, the man whose generalship had won the final victory; "the man who, greater than Cæsar, had held a kingly crown within reach and had refused it." His election was unanimous. For Vice-President the choice fell upon John Adams of Massachusetts.

THOMPSON, THE CLERK OF CONGRESS, ANNOUNCES TO WASHINGTON HIS ELECTION TO THE PRESIDENCY

Charles Thompson, since 1774 the secretary of the Continental Congress, arrived at Mount Vernon on April 14th, and there in the reception room of the old mansion he announced to Washington his election as the first President of the United States.

"Two days later," Bassett records in his *The Federalist System*, "the President-elect set out for New York. A mile from his home he was met by an escort from Alexandria; at the Potomac's bank he was turned over by these to an escort from Georgetown; and thus he was passed on by Georgetown to Baltimore, thence to Philadelphia, thence through New Jersey to New York; so that he was never, during the whole journey, without a suitable guard of honor. Children and women strewed flowers in his road. . . . and at the dock on Manhattan Island he was received with the wildest expressions of joy."

THE FIRST INAUGURATION

"The inauguration," according to Irving's *Life of Washington*, "took place on the 30th of April. At nine o'clock in the morning there were religious services in all the churches, and prayers put up for the blessing of Heaven on the new government. At twelve o'clock the city troops paraded before Washington's door, and soon after the committees of Congress and heads of departments came in their carriages. At half-past twelve the procession moved forward, preceded by the troops; next came the committees and heads of departments in their carriages; then Washington in a coach of state, his aid-de-camp, Colonel Humphreys, and his secretary, Mr. Lear, in his own carriage. The foreign ministers and a long train of citizens brought up the rear.

[270]

Thompson, the Clerk of Congress, Announcing
to Washington, at Mount Vernon, His Election
to the Presidency

Illustration from
THE FIRST PRESIDENT OF THE UNITED STATES
by Woodrow Wilson
Originally published in
HARPER'S MAGAZINE, *November,* 1896

"About two hundred yards before reaching the hall, Washington and his suite alighted from their carriages and passed through the troops, who were drawn up on each side, into the hall and Senate chamber where the Vice-President, the Senate, and the House of Representatives were assembled. The Vice-President, John Adams, recently inaugurated, advanced and conducted Washington to a chair of state at the upper end of the room. A solemn silence prevailed when the Vice-President rose and informed him that all things were prepared for him to take the oath of office required by the Constitution.

"The oath was to be administered by the chancellor of the state of New York in a balcony in front of the Senate chamber, and in full view of an immense multitude occupying the street, the windows, and even roofs of the adjacent houses. The balcony formed a kind of open recess, with lofty columns supporting the roof. In the center was a table with a covering of crimson velvet, upon which lay a superbly bound bible on a crimson-velvet cushion. This was all the paraphernalia that had been provided for this august scene.

"All eyes were fixed upon the balcony when, at the appointed hour, Washington made his appearance, accompanied by various public functionaries and members of the Senate and House of Representatives. He was clad in a full suit of dark-brown cloth, of American manufacture, with a steel-hilted dress sword, white-silk stockings, and silver shoe buckles. His hair was dressed and powdered in the fashion of the day, and worn in a bag and solitaire.

"His entrance on the balcony was hailed by universal shouts. He was evidently moved by this demonstration of public affection. Advancing to the front of the balcony, he laid his hand upon his heart, bowed several times, and then retreated to an armchair near the table. The populace appeared to understand that the scene had overcome him, and were hushed at once into profound silence.

"After a few moments Washington rose and again came forward. John Adams, the Vice-President, stood on his right;

Washington Met by His Neighbors on His Way
to the Inauguration

Illustration from
WASHINGTON'S INAUGURATION
by John Bach McMaster

Originally published in
HARPER'S MAGAZINE, *April*, 1889

The Inaugural Procession

Illustration from
BUILDING THE NATION
by Charles Carleton Coffin

Originally published by
HARPER & BROTHERS, 1883

The Inauguration

Illustration from
WASHINGTON'S INAUGURATION
by John Bach McMaster

Originally published in
HARPER'S MAGAZINE, *April*, 1889

on his left the chancellor of the state, Robert R. Livingston; somewhat in the rear were Roger Sherman, Alexander Hamilton, Generals Knox, St. Clair, the Baron Steuben, and others.

"The chancellor advanced to administer the oath prescribed by the Constitution, and Mr. Otis, the secretary of the Senate, held up the bible on its crimson cushion. The oath was read slowly and distinctly, Washington at the same time laying his hand on the open bible. When it was concluded, he replied, solemnly, 'I swear—so help me, God!' Mr. Otis would have raised the bible to his lips, but he bowed down reverently and kissed it.

"The chancellor now stepped forward, waved his hand, and exclaimed, 'Long live George Washington, President of the United States!' At this moment a flag was displayed on the cupola of the hall; on which signal there was a general discharge of artillery on the Battery, all the bells in the city rang out a joyful peal, and the multitude rent the air with acclamations.

"Washington again bowed to the people and returned into the Senate chamber, where he delivered to both Houses of Congress his inaugural address, characterized by his usual modesty, moderation, and good sense, but uttered with a voice deep, slightly tremulous, and so low as to demand close attention in the listeners. He then proceeded with the assemblage to St. Paul's Church, where prayers were read by Doctor Prevost, Bishop of the Protestant Episcopal Church in New York, who had been appointed by the Senate one of the chaplains of Congress. So closed the ceremonies of the inauguration.

CELEBRATION ON THE NIGHT OF THE INAUGURATION

"The whole day was one of sincere rejoicing, and in the evening there were brilliant illuminations and fireworks."

At the very beginning of Washington's administration, the question of what title should be used in addressing him became a matter of much concern to certain members of the government. The House, following the designation given in the Constitution,

Celebration on the Night of the Inauguration

Illustration from
WASHINGTON'S INAUGURATION
by John Bach McMaster

Originally published in
HARPER'S MAGAZINE, *April,* 1889

proposed to call him "The President of the United States," while the Senate was in favor of "His Highness, the President of the United States of America, and Protector of their Liberties." Many other titles, more or less suggestive of royalty, were proposed, but finally the Senate, accepting the idea of the House, adopted "Mr. President' as his title. And ever since that time the ruler of what has become the greatest nation on earth is known simply as "Mr. President."

It was natural that the first President, as well as those that have followed him, should be overrun with callers. Even people who had business that could have been attended to by subordinates insisted on seeing Washington. The President must have time in which to discharge his official duties. Accordingly, Washington announced that on Tuesdays, from three to four in the afternoon, he would hold public receptions, or levees, as they were then called, and that all others who had business to transact with the President would have to make appointments in advance.

On Friday evenings Mrs. Washington held informal receptions. Washington was always present on these occasions, mingling with the company, but always maintaining a precise dignity, paying courtly compliments to the ladies, and never going beyond bowing and smiling to the gentlemen.

ORGANIZING THE NEW GOVERNMENT

During Washington's first administration his energies, as well as those of Congress, were chiefly devoted to the work of organizing the government of the United States under the Constitution. In every state there were many who felt that the Constitution had made the states too weak and the Federal government too strong. The measures passed by Congress, among them the funding of the debt of the old Continental Congress, the assumption and funding of the debts contracted by the states during the Revolution, Hamilton's proposal to stamp on the coins the head of the President, served to give the idea that the country was drifting toward monarchy. Moreover, Washington's stiff and formal ceremonious-

At Mrs. Washington's Reception

Illustration from
OUR COUNTRY'S CRADLE
by Thomas Wentworth Higginson

Originally published in
HARPER'S MAGAZINE, *February,* 1884

ness in his official intercourse, as well as the almost regal style in which he appeared in public, together with the stately weekly levees, greatly strengthened this notion in the minds of the ultra-democrats. That this feeling had taken deep root was shown in the presidential election of 1792. In that contest Washington was again chosen unanimously, but the Republican party, only just organized by Thomas Jefferson, won fifty of the one hundred and thirty-two electoral votes cast, for George Clinton, their candidate for Vice-President.

Jefferson's new party owed its rapid growth to the partiality and sympathy of its members for French republicanism, which, with the outbreak of the French Revolution in 1789, had swept the United States in one great wave of enthusiasm. It was natural that the struggle of the French people for political freedom should excite interest and sympathy among the Americans, who felt that the uprising in France was the direct result of their own quite recent example. Jefferson and his followers saw that the French had already done exactly what they were trying to do—to exalt the rights of the individual at the expense of a strong central government of the monarchical type, which they were convinced Hamilton and the Federalists were attempting to establish in the United States. Thus the French Revolution caused a more distinct defining of party lines between the Federalists and the Republicans. The Federalists, led by Hamilton, hated democracy and had no sympathy for the French, while the Republicans, led by Jefferson, were filled with enthusiasm at the progress of events in France. Hamilton had once declared the people to be "a great beast," while Jefferson placed such faith in them that he said at the time of Shays's Rebellion: "I am persuaded that the good sense of the people will always be found the best army. They may be led astray for a moment, but will soon correct themselves." And referring to the French Revolution, he wrote, "Rather than it should have failed, I would have seen half the earth desolated; were there but an Adam and Eve left in every country, and left free, it would be better than it is now."

The News of the Execution of Louis XVI

Illustration from
WASHINGTON AND THE FRENCH CRAZE OF '93
by John Bach McMaster

Originally published in
Harper's Magazine, *April*, 1897

THE NEWS OF THE EXECUTION OF LOUIS XVI

Such was the state of affairs in the two opposing political camps when news of the execution of Louis XVI, in January, 1793, brought a pause to the mad frenzy with which the Americans had been celebrating the great victories of Dumouriez over the allied armies under the Duke of Brunswick. Then, two months later, came news of a more serious kind—the news that the French Republic had declared war against England.

War between France and Great Britain was a dreadful thing for the people of the United States to think of. Bound as they were to France by two treaties, one of amity and commerce and one of alliance, it probably meant that their country would be called on to take up arms in the cause of France; and this was quite enough to calm the ardor of the less violent Republicans. The same ship that had brought these alarming tidings had also made known that a minister from the French Republic was already on his way to Philadelphia. Washington immediately summoned his Cabinet. As France was to wage an offensive war, it was decided that the United States should remain neutral, the alliance with France being a purely defensive one. It was also decided to receive the French minister when he arrived.

CITIZEN GENÊT FORMALLY PRESENTED TO WASHINGTON

"Citizen Genêt, the minister from the French Republic," according to *Harper's Encyclopædia of United States History*, "landed at Charleston, South Carolina, April 9th, 1793. He was received with open arms by the Republican, or Democratic, party, in spite of the attitude taken by Washington. He was disposed to treat the United States government with contempt, believing the people would not sustain it in its coldness toward the French revolutionists. He came with blank commissions for naval and military service, and before he proceeded to the seat of government to present his credentials he fitted out two privateers at Charleston to prey on British commerce, and gave authority to every French consul in America to constitute himself a court of admiralty to dispose of

A Banquet to Genêt

Illustration from
WASHINGTON AND THE FRENCH CRAZE OF '93
by John Bach McMaster

Originally published in
HARPER'S MAGAZINE, *April,* 1897

Women at the Polls in New Jersey

In New Jersey in the period 1790-1807, women were permitted to vote, and many of them took great pride in doing so. It is probable that this is the earliest instance of voting in government elections by English-speaking women in America.

Illustration from
WOMEN AT THE POLLS IN NEW JERSEY IN THE GOOD OLD TIMES
Originally published in
HARPER'S WEEKLY, *November 12, 1880*

prizes brought into American ports by French cruisers. One of these vessels, *L'Embuscade*, went prowling up the coast, seizing several small vessels, finally capturing a British merchantman within the capes of the Delaware, when she proceeded in triumph to Philadelphia, where she was received with acclamations of joy by the excited people. Upon the bow of *L'Embuscade*, her foremast, and her stern, liberty caps were conspicuous, and the British colors were reversed on the prize, with the French colors flying above them. Fourteen days later Genêt arrived by land at Philadelphia, where, according to a preconcerted plan, a number of citizens met him at the Schuylkill and escorted him into the city, while cannon

From *Harper's Magazine*, April, 1897

ARRIVAL OF GENÊT AT GRAY'S FERRY

roared and church bells rang out peals of welcome. There he received addresses from various societies, and so anxious were his admirers to do homage to the representative of the authors of the Reign of Terror in France that they invited him to a public dinner before he had presented his credentials to the President of the United States.

Genêt presented his credentials to Washington in person April 19, 1793, and found himself in an atmosphere of the most profound dignity. He felt his own littleness as a mere political enthusiast

Citizen Genêt Formally Presented to Washington

Illustration from
WASHINGTON AND THE FRENCH CRAZE OF '93
by John Bach McMaster

Originally published in
HARPER'S MAGAZINE, *April,* 1897

while standing before the representative of true democracy in America and of the soundest principles of the American republic. He withdrew from the audience abashed and subdued. He had heard expressions of sincere regard for the people of France that touched the sensibilities of his heart, and he had felt, in the courtesy and severe simplicity and frankness of the President's manner, wholly free from effervescent enthusiasm, a withering rebuke not only of the adulators in public places, but also of his own pretensions, aspirations, and offensive conduct. Once out of the presence of Washington, he became the same defiant champion of the 'rights of the people,' affecting to be shocked at the evidences of monarchical sympathies in the President's house. He there saw a bust of Louis XVI, and declared its presence in the house of the President of the United States was an 'insult to France,' and he was 'astonished' to find that relatives of Lafayette had lately been admitted to the presence of the President.

BANQUET TO GENÊT AT OELLER'S TAVERN, PHILADELPHIA

"His feelings were soothed at a great banquet given him by his Republican friends at Oeller's Tavern, Philadelphia, May 23, 1793, where his ears were greeted with the 'Marseilles' hymn and his eyes delighted with a 'tree of liberty' on the table. His heart was made glad by having the red cap of liberty placed on his own head first and then upon the head of each guest, while the wearer, under the inspiration of its symbolism, uttered some patriotic sentiment. At the dinner, at which Governor Mifflin of Pennsylvania was present, a roasted pig received the name of the murdered French king, and the head, severed from the body, was carried around to each of the guests, who, after placing the cap of liberty on his own head, pronounced the word 'tyrant,' and proceeded to mangle with his knife that of the poor pig. One of the Republican taverns in Philadelphia displayed as a sign a revolting picture of the mutilated and blood-stained corpse of Queen Marie Antoinette.

"This madness ran a short course and its victims became heartily ashamed of it. Genêt took this for a genuine and settled feeling

Washington in the Garden at Mount Vernon

Illustration from
FIRST IN PEACE
by Woodrow Wilson

Originally published in
HARPER'S MAGAZINE, *September,* 1896

and acted upon it. Meanwhile the insulted government took most dignified action. The captured British merchantman was restored to its owners and the privateers were ordered out of American waters. Orders were sent to the collectors at all American ports to seize all vessels fitted out as privateers and to prevent the sale of any prize captured by such vessels. Chief-Justice Jay declared it to be the duty of grand juries to present all persons guilty of such violation of the laws of nations with respect to any of the belligerent powers. The French ambassador and his friends were greatly irritated. He protested, and Secretary of State Jefferson, who had favored the enthusiasm of Genêt's reception, finding he had a troublesome friend on his hands, plainly told Genêt that by commissioning privateers he had violated the sovereignty of the United States. With offensive pertinacity, Genêt denied this doctrine as contrary to right, justice, and the laws of nations, and threatened to 'appeal from the President to the people;' and in this the Republican newspapers sustained him. Secret Democratic societies which had been formed became more bold and active, and Genêt, mistaking the popular clamor for the deliberate voice of the nation, actually undertook to fit out a privateer at Philadelphia, in defiance of the government, during the President's absence at Mount Vernon. It was a vessel captured by *L'Embuscade*, and Genêt named her *The Little Democrat*.

"Governor Mifflin, like Jefferson, had become sick of the 'Citizen,' and he interfered. Genêt would not heed his threats nor the persuasion of Jefferson. He denounced the President as unfaithful to the wishes of the people, and resolved to force him to call Congress together. Washington, on his return to Philadelphia, when informed of the insolence of Genêt, exclaimed, 'Is the minister of the French Republic to set the acts of the government at defiance with impunity?' His Cabinet answered, 'No!' The most exacting country could not counsel longer forbearance, and the French government was requested, July, 1793, to recall its minister. There was a reaction in the public mind toward a more patriotic attitude. The insolence of Genêt had shocked the national pride.

Washington and Nellie Custis

Illustration from
THE FIRST PRESIDENT OF THE UNITED STATES
by Woodrow Wilson

Originally published in
HARPER'S MAGAZINE, *November*, 1896

On April 22, 1793, the President issued a proclamation of neutrality, which the radical Democrats denounced as an 'edict of royalty.'"

"Genêt's recall," writes Bassett in *The Federalist System*, "was accompanied with circumstances peculiarly unfortunate for him. The Robespierre faction, which was now supreme in France, hated him because he was identified with the discarded Girondins. His successor, Fauchet, brought orders to arrest him, and send him back to France to be tried for malversation in office. Washington, disliking to press him to this extremity, refused to allow him to be extradited, and thus probably saved his life. He remained in America and married a daughter of Governor Clinton of New York, where he lived to old age."

Toward the end of his fourth year as the first President of the United States Washington had declared that he would not stand for re-election. Indeed, he was on the point of issuing a farewell address like that which he gave to his countrymen four years later. But Jefferson and Hamilton, the leaders of the two opposing political parties, making it clear to him that the nation needed his services for four years more, he consented to stand again.

WASHINGTON AT MOUNT VERNON

With the ending of his second term, however, Washington made it definitely known that he would not accept office again. His refusal was due mostly to the disgust with which he was filled at the continued attacks which the Republicans had heaped upon him, although the wish to pass his remaining days in the quiet of his Virginia home greatly influenced him. At length his longing for rest and retirement was gratified and he was soon at his beloved Mount Vernon. There, with Mrs. Washington and his adopted daughter, Nellie Custis, whom he had adopted as a child at her father's death and brought up with the most affectionate care, he found happiness and contentment until his death, December 14, 1799, less than three years after he had given up the cares of office.

Death of Washington

Illustration from
THE FIRST PRESIDENT OF THE UNITED STATES
by Woodrow Wilson

Originally published in
HARPER'S MAGAZINE, *November,* 1896

As Woodrow Wilson says in his *Life of Washington:* "The country knew him when he was dead; knew the majesty, the nobility, the unsullied greatness of the man who was gone, and knew not whether to mourn or give praise. He could not serve them any more; but they saw his light shine already upon the future as upon the past, and were glad."

Chapter V

THE SECOND WAR FOR INDEPENDENCE

ENÊT'S foolish and insolent behavior toward Washington, resulting in his recall, also lost him the favor of the people; and with the collapse of his popularity the curtain was rung down on the last act of the French craze in America. In consequence, however, of our neutral position during the war between France and England—first while France was a republic and later when Napoleon became Emperor—our relations with both countries became strained. During this whole period American politics was almost completely dominated by the issue of events in Europe, and party lines were sharply drawn between those who clung to the past and those who looked to the future. The former were known as the Federalists, who sympathized with England and hated France; the latter as the Democrats, or Republicans, who looked with interest and sympathy upon the French Revolution as directly the result of their own struggle for liberty, among whom sentimental feelings were still aroused at the memory of the French alliance, while for England their hearts were filled with hatred.

Due to the existence of these English and French factions in American politics, the development of the nation was greatly hampered. But with the War of 1812 came a new generation of men and women who turned their eyes away from Europe and the old colonial dependence; who, thrusting the old leaders aside, themselves took the leadership and, all unprepared and rent with faction as it was, led the country into the war by which the United States shook off forever the incubus of European domination and became really a "free, sovereign, and independent" nation, which, when James Madison became President in 1809, it was in name only.

Thus the causes of the Second War for Independence, as the War of 1812 is truly called, had their rise during the years following 1793, when France and England were at each other's throats. "Between the millstones of English orders and French decrees," Presidents Adams, Jefferson, and Madison had "seen the freedom of American commerce, the honor of the nation, and the safety of its citizens ground to dust." Embargo and Nonintercourse Acts had been resorted to in the hope of gaining freedom for American commerce, but these methods of "peaceful war" were without avail. The new Congress, however, chosen in 1810 and meeting in extra session, November 4, 1811, was composed of men of the new generation—young men of fresh courage, who had unbounded faith in the Republic's strength and future. They had for leaders such men as Henry Clay and John C. Calhoun, who, imbued with the American spirit, turned their backs on the past and, scorning the temporizing spirit that had guided our foreign relations since the time of Jefferson, led his successor and their party out on to the broad American highway upon which all signboards pointed to the future.

IMPRESSMENT OF AMERICAN SEAMEN

To the minds of Clay and Calhoun war with Great Britain already existed, for, as Clay declared to the House, "Is it not equivalent to invasion if the mouths of our harbors and outlets are

A Scene in Cortlandt Street, New York,
in 1793

*An old money-lender spying upon his niece and her
lover, whose suit he did not approve.*

Illustration from
THE MYSTERIOUS CHEST
by Howard Pyle

Originally published in
HARPER'S MAGAZINE, *December, 1908*

Impressment of American Seamen

Illustration from
OUR COUNTRY'S CRADLE
by Thomas Wentworth Higginson

Originally published in
HARPER'S MAGAZINE, *April*, 1884

blocked up and we are denied egress from our own waters? Or when a burglar is at our door shall we bravely sally forth and repel his felonious entrance, or meanly skulk within the cells of the castle?"

Still President Madison, who loved peace, as had Jefferson before him, hesitated to follow the war Republicans. When, however, Great Britain refused to rescind her orders in council in regard to the blockade until France unconditionally withdrew her decrees; when the British Foreign Minister followed this up with the statement that to yield to the American demands would be "utterly subversive of the most important and indisputable maritime rights of the British Empire," Madison, despairing of a peaceful issue, on June 1, 1812, sent a message to Congress urging a declaration of war, and two weeks later, June 18th, when Congress declared war against Great Britain, the so-called Jeffersonian system came to an end and a new epoch in the history of the United States was ushered in.

As Professor Channing says in his admirable work, *The Jeffersonian System*, "Inciting the Indians to rebellion, impressing American seamen and making them serve on British warships, closing the ports of Europe to American commerce, these were the counts in the indictment against the people and government of Great Britain. Yet there would have been no war had not other factors come into play. The British still looked upon Americans as provincials who were dependent upon Great Britain for their well-being. They assumed a patronizing tone, which ill-fitted the statesmen of a country which had been forced to concede independence, in saying, for example, that the Americans, generally speaking, 'were not a people we should be proud to acknowledge as our relations.'"

1800.

PRIVATEERS AND PRIVATEERSMEN

In New England, where the Federalists were strong, the war

was denounced as "Mr. Madison's war." Its unpopularity in that section was shown by the refusal of the governors of Massachusetts, Connecticut, and New Hampshire to order out their militia beyond the bounds of their respective states. In the early period, therefore, much went wrong. The reverses that befell the American army during 1812 spread gloom over the people, justified the warnings of the opposition, and increased the activity and machinations of the peace party. To the surprise of all, however, it was upon the sea, not the land, that the United States proved eminently successful, and the victory of the *Constitution* over the *Guerrière* was the first of a long line of triumphs. These naval victories astounded the British public. The lion was bearded in his den. The claims of Great Britain to the mastery of the seas were vehemently and practically disputed. Nor were the naval triumphs of the Americans confined to the national vessels. Privateers swarmed on the oceans in the summer and autumn of 1812, and were making prizes in every direction. Most of these were sent out from the sections of the country where the opposition to the war was the strongest— from Salem, Boston, New York, Philadelphia, and Baltimore. "But," quoting from Babcock's *Rise of American Nationality*, "the combined motives of necessity, plunder, and revenge soon overcame all scruples. . . . Idle vessels, idle pilot boats, and idle sailors, the result of British orders and French decrees and American embargoes and Nonintercourse Acts, found immediate occupation. The vessels themselves had been built to evade British cruisers; they were fast-sailing, easily handled craft, and over and over again demonstrated that it took more than one cruiser to catch and hold them. The very names themselves indicate something of the spirit prompting this form of attack upon British interest: *Orders in Council; The Right of Search; Bunker Hill; True-Blooded Yankee; United We Stand.* A month after the declaration of war, sixty-five privateers were in search of British merchantmen; and within six months three hundred prizes had been taken by public and private vessels of the United States. Niles's *Weekly Register* from the beginning of the war until late in 1814 published a regular list of American prizes, and maintained steadily as a heading for the list, as it mounted up past the thousand mark, this quotation from the *British Naval Register:*

> 'The winds and seas are Britain's wide domain,
> And not a sail, but by permission, spreads.' "

COLONIAL PRIVATEERS

Let us here briefly mention the privateering of the earlier Colonial period. Thomas A. Janvier, writing in *Harper's Magazine,* February, 1895, on "New York Colonial Privateers," says, "Of all the lines along which the sea wealth of New York was won in

From *Harper's Magazine,* February, 1895
NEW YORK COLONIAL PRIVATEERS

Colonial times the first place should be given to privateering." Although out-and-out piracy was better while it lasted, and slave trading also was profitable, as an all-around industry, privateering ranked first of all, having plenty of fight in it and plenty of cash flowing out of it.

Again quoting from Mr. Janvier's article: "Quite the most distinct of these half-real, half-imaginary figures which rise up from the depths of our sea-fighting past is Capt. Regnier Tongrelow of the *New York Galley,* who probably was a great scamp with all the making of a pirate inside his privateering veneer, but whose fighting

Captain Tongrelow Took the Biggest

Illustration from
NEW YORK COLONIAL PRIVATEERS
by Thomas A. Janvier

Originally published in
HARPER'S MAGAZINE, *February*, 1895

qualities truly were of a sort to warm one's heart." Tongrelow's prizes were many and fat; and such was his zest that he would give chase to the biggest of ships; for fighting against odds did not deter him. In a news-letter of 1706 it is recorded that Tongrelow, being "off Cape Franswa in company with two Jamaica privateers and one of Curaçoa, they espyed 5 sail and gave Chase"; and then as always Captain Tongrelow took the biggest.

Not only were these privateersmen a terror to their enemies afloat, but also to their friends ashore. However much New York gloried in their deeds at sea, they stood in great fear of these men, once they came ashore, inclined as they were to get drunk and while in that state ready to fight everybody who came along.

"Probably the worst of these riots," says Janvier in the article already referred to, "occurred in September, 1705, and the news-letter of September 24th, in which it is chronicled, begins with the statement that 'on the 18th Instant arrived here a small Prize Sloop taken by Capt. Penniston, loaded with wine and brandy.' The writer of the letter, who does not seem to perceive any connection between the arrival of this sloopload of potential drunkenness and the disturbance which within twenty-four hours followed it, continues:

"'On the 19th instant, about 10 at night, some Privateers began a Riot before the Sheriff's House of this City, assaulted the Sheriff at his door without any provocation, and beat and wounded several persons that came to his assistance, and in a few minutes the Privateers tumultuously met together in great numbers, upon which Forces were sent out of the Fort to suppress them, . . . but before these Forces could meet with them, the Privateers unhappily met Lieut. Wharton Featherstone Hough and Ensign Alcock . . . and barborously murdered the first and greviously wounded the latter.'" Finally, after severe fighting some of the privateers were taken prisoners by "Seamen of Her Majesties Ships." And truly, as the writer, commenting upon privateersmen in general, says in conclusion, "'It would be tedious to relate the particulars, but their insolence is beyond expression.'"

Carrying Powder to Perry at Lake Erie

Illustration from
The Original Painting
by Howard Pyle

Made for the Du Pont Powder Company,
Wilmington, Delaware

Barbarously Murdered the First, and Grievously
Wounded the Latter

Illustration from
NEW YORK COLONIAL PRIVATEERS
by Thomas A. Janvier

Originally published in
HARPER'S MAGAZINE, *February*, 1895

Such were the privateersmen of the early Colonial times. It is most gratifying, however, to know that the privateersmen who made the reputation of the American navy in the first year of the War of 1812 were of quite another stamp—that navy which was to win even greater glory the next year in the war on the Lakes, the control of which was so important to both contestants.

CARRYING POWDER TO LAKE ERIE FOR COMMODORE PERRY

The work of constructing a fleet upon Lake Erie was assigned to Capt. Oliver Hazard Perry, who at the time was in charge of gunboat service at Newport. "When," as Babcock says in his *Rise of American Nationality*, "Perry reached Presqu'isle, now known as Erie, the ship carpenters had on the stocks two twenty-gun brigs, a schooner, and three gunboats. With the exception of timber, nearly everything had to be brought by slow and difficult transportation from Philadelphia by way of Pittsburgh. So came the iron, guns, ammunition, sails, cordage, and provisions. . . . Through the summer of 1813 the work went on vigorously, and when the British fleet, moved by lack of provisions, attacked Perry in September, his improvised fleet, created by capture, purchase, and construction, consisted of six vessels, which in tonnage, men, and metal outranked the British." Perry's victory over the British, September 10, 1813, immortalized by two phrases—Lawrence's "Don't give up the Ship," displayed on the flag which flew from the masthead of Perry's flagship, the *Lawrence*, and his own laconic dispatch, "We have met the enemy and they are ours"—not only gave control of Lake Erie to the United States, but rendered a British invasion of American territory impossible, while it offered to the Americans a strong possibility of a successful invasion of Canada.

Foiled in their attempt of invasion at the north, the British now turned their attention to the south, and in August, 1814, captured Washington. After burning the Capitol and other public buildings, they withdrew toward Baltimore, which was to be their next prey; but there the people themselves took charge of the

A Privateersman Ashore

Illustration from
THE EVOLUTION OF NEW YORK
by Thomas A. Janvier

Originally published in
HARPER'S MAGAZINE, *June, 1893*

defense and the British army was beaten off. Afterward, in January, 1815, came the victory of New Orleans, where Andrew Jackson's riflemen drove back the British army with a total loss of more than two thousand against an American loss of seventy-one.

This glorious victory, won two weeks after the treaty of peace had been actually signed, was most gratifying to the American people. This triumph brought to an end Benjamin Franklin's war

From *Harper's Magazine*, November, 1879

ARRIVAL OF THE COACH AT AN OLD STAGE STATION ON THE NATIONAL ROAD

for independence, who, after the victory at Yorktown was known, is said to have reproved an acquaintance who referred to the Revolution as the war of independence by saying: "Sir, you mean the *Revolution;* the war of *independence* is yet to come. The Revolution was a war *for* independence not *of* independence." And this was truly so, for until 1815 America was like a ship in a storm, veering this way and that as the winds blew from Europe. But at last,

[304]

When All the World Seemed Young

Originally published in
Harper's Magazine, *August,* 1909

as Babcock says, "like the ship in Kipling's story, the nation found itself." The "Signing of the Declaration of Independence," Gaillard Hunt writes in his *Life in America One Hundred Years Ago*, "had marked the beginning of the nation; the signing of the Treaty of Ghent marked the beginning of its strong, vigorous manhood." In finding itself the nation also found new leaders, and most important among them was Andrew Jackson, who after 1815 became known as the "Hero of New Orleans."

WHEN ALL THE WORLD SEEMED YOUNG

Meanwhile James Monroe succeeded Madison as President, and the eight years of his administration are known as the "Era of Good Feeling"; for what with the sixteen years of bitter political strife that had raged since 1800, the placid years of Monroe's rule seemed to have ushered in a golden age—years of happiness and prosperity when all the world seemed young again. Yet Monroe's own Cabinet was filled with rival presidential candidates, among them John Quincy Adams, whose election in 1824 again aroused the most bitter political warfare.

With the close of the War of 1812 the young Republic had thrown off every vestige that smacked of colonial dependence. Henceforth it was to go forth arrayed in the garments of independence, to lower its flag to no nation, to assert its predominance in the western continent; and in the famous Monroe doctrine to give notice to the Old World to keep its hands off the American continent. This spirit of nationalism was shown not only in its foreign relations, but also in the unbounded vigor with which the nation as a whole set out to develop the resources upon which the future of the country depended.

Nothing was of more importance to the nation's progress than an improved transportation system. To open and develop the country, especially the West, toward which a great migration had now set in, roads and canals were necessary. Jefferson in 1806 had recommended the building of a national road, and by 1818 the National Road, popularly known as the "Old National Pike," had been built from Cumberland on the Potomac, across the mountains to Wheeling on the Ohio. Although Monroe strongly recommended a system of interstate highways and canals, he vetoed a bill giving the national government this power, on the ground that it encroached on the rights of the individual states. But in the administration of John Quincy Adams, which began in 1825, these projects for internal improvements were put into effect and a great system of roads and canals were built for the nation as a whole.

OPENING OF THE ERIE CANAL, JULY 4, 1825

In recommending Congress to appropriate money for these purposes President Adams cited the example of the great Erie Canal, which New York had built as a state enterprise and thrown open July 4, 1825. The Erie Canal was first proposed by Gouverneur Morris in 1777, but "it is," as Turner writes in his *Rise of the New West*, "the glory of De Witt Clinton that he saw the economic revolution which the Erie Canal would work, and that he was able to present clearly and effectively the reasons which made the undertaking practicable and the financial plan which made it possible." He saw it begun during his first administration. The first excavation was made July 4, 1817, and it was completed and formally opened by him, as chief magistrate of the state, July 4, 1825, when a grand aquatic procession from Albany proceeded to the sea, and the Governor poured a keg of the water of Lake Erie into the Atlantic Ocean. This canal connected the waters of the Great Lakes with the Atlantic Ocean by way of the Hudson River.

THE OLD NATIONAL PIKE

In this same year Congress had provided for the extension of the Old National Pike from Wheeling to Zanesville, Ohio. Annual appropriations continued to be made for the road, and by 1833 it was completed as far as Columbus, Ohio.

When General Jackson, in 1829, journeyed from Nashville to Washington to take his seat as President of the United States, he traveled by stage-coach over this famous old road. In those happy

Opening of the Erie Canal

Illustration from
THE EVOLUTION OF NEW YORK
by Thomas A. Janvier
Originally published in
HARPER'S MAGAZINE, *June*, 1893

coaching days no other post road in the country did such a thriving business as this fine old highway which was the means of opening up the West and the Southwest to the East. It was excellently macadamized; the distances were marked by iron mile posts and

From *Harper's Magazine*, November, 1879

AN OLD GOVERNMENT TOLLGATE, WITH WESTWARD-BOUND EXPRESS, ON THE "OLD NATIONAL PIKE"

nearly every mile had its tavern, at which the travelers would alight from the stage, sure to find the best of food and drink. Most of the travelers were farmers and stock raisers of the West, but statesmen on their way to Washington were frequently met with. Nor were these Solons averse to tarrying awhile at the taverns,

General Jackson, President-elect, on His Way to
Washington

Illustration from
A PRESIDENTIAL PROGRESS
Originally published in
HARPER'S WEEKLY, *March 12,* 1881

chatting affably with the guests, and, upon leaving, giving them the handshake of fellowship.

PRESIDENT-ELECT JACKSON ON HIS WAY TO WASHINGTON

The wagons were so numerous on the Old National Pike that the leaders of one team had their noses in the trough at the end of the next wagon ahead; and the coaches, drawn by four or six horses, dashed along at a great rate of speed. Besides the coaches and wagons there were gentlemen traveling singly on horseback, with

From *Harper's Weekly*, November, 1879

A COMPLIMENTARY ADDRESS TO OLD HICKORY

all the accouterments of their journey packed in saddle bags. General Jackson's journey over this road as President-elect was like a royal progress. Everywhere along the route he was greeted by enthusiastic crowds, and was frequently called upon for a speech, which the stately and courtly old "Hero of New Orleans" would deliver from the driver's seat. At every stopping place along the road he was called upon to address impromptu meetings which the magic of his military and political renown had called together.

The Second War for Independence

A great career was before this man who, writes Higginson in his *History of the United States*, "was called 'Old Hickory' by three-quarters of the nation; and who made 'Hurrah for Jackson!' a cry so potent that it had the force of a decree." With his election democracy was triumphant and the people asserted their right to govern themselves. "Jackson's election," writes MacDonald in his *Jacksonian Democracy*, "was all this and more. To personal vindication of Jackson was added emphatic popular indorsement of the social and political order with which he was identified. In the election of Jackson the people of the United States turned their backs on their early principles of statesmanship and intrusted the conduct of the Federal government to an untrained, self-willed, passionate frontier soldier. That he was not of the old school was, in the eyes of his supporters, a commendation. It was as idle then as it is now to bemoan a change. A great democracy will never be governed for long together by its best men, but by its average. To the average voter in 1828 Jackson was a great popular leader because they held him to be also a typical democrat. With him, democracy springs into the saddle. It had yet to show how well it could ride."

The election of Andrew Jackson to the Presidency marks the beginning of the third great epoch in the history of the United States—the beginning of personal politics, the overthrow of the old statesmanship that had reigned since the days of the Revolution, and the founding of a national democracy built upon the idea of the sovereignty of the people. To the very end of "the reign of King Andrew," as the eight years of his rule have been so fittingly termed, he never lost his popularity with the masses of the people, whose will he claimed to be the unerring interpreter. For them, in turn, his will was law; all that he did met with their approbation; their sympathy and support were warmly given him on every issue; and when, at the close of his term, he asked them to support Martin Van Buren, his candidate for the Presidency, the people rallied to his support and by electing Van Buren gave to Jackson his last and greatest triumph.

[311]

Before the curtain had rung down on Jackson's "reign" a new
issue had loomed up on the horizon—a most ominous one, the
slavery question, which was brought prominently before the public

From *Harper's Magazine*, November, 1879]

AN OLD WAYSIDE TAVERN ON THE OLD NATIONAL PIKE

[312]

of the North and the South in 1831, by the negro insurrection in Virginia led by Nat Turner and the establishment of the *Liberator* in Boston by William Lloyd Garrison, the great abolitionist. Although there was a rising sentiment against slavery in the North, the attitude of the people there on the whole was against the abolitionists, with whose demands for the unconditional emancipation of all slaves they were not yet in full sympathy. Indeed, but slight attention seems to have been paid in the North even to the actual violation of the Missouri Compromise, when, in 1836, by act of Congress, a large stretch of land was taken from the region which the Compromise of 1820 had declared to be forever free, and added to the slave state of Missouri.

The abolitionists, however, were persistent and their continued agitation finally brought the slavery question to an issue in the halls of Congress, where the aggressive attitude of the Southern members, under the leadership of Calhoun, was the means of causing a great change in the sentiment of the North. From 1836 onward the abolitionists swamped Congress with petitions demanding the freeing of the negroes. They also distributed through the mails a great quantity of literature in which the moral and constitutional aspect of slavery was held up to obloquy. All this greatly alarmed the South, and the slaveholders' representatives in Congress succeeded in passing a "gag rule" by which all petitions relating in any way to slavery or the slave trade should "be laid on the table and that no further action shall be taken thereon." But former President John Quincy Adams, then a representative from Massachusetts, protested, declaring the right to petition Congress sacred and the resolution prohibiting it "a direct violation of the Constitution of the United States, of the rules of this House, and of the rights of my constituents."

This attempt of the Southerners to prevent a discussion of slavery on the floor of Congress only placed another weapon in the hands of the abolitionists, who now retorted that a subject which could not be safely discussed in the Congress of the United States was an institution harmful to the country. From that time on most of the memorials to Congress were sent in the care of this venerable champion of the right of petition, who continued his warfare against the "gag rule" for nearly ten years, until it was finally repealed. "Gag resolutions" were also passed by the Senate, where Calhoun, in speaking of the petitions, declared them to be "a foul slander on nearly one-half of the states of the Union." As to the matter of slavery, he vehemently declared that "it had grown with our growth and strengthened with our strength. It has entered into and modified our institutions, civil and political. None other can be substituted." Continuing, he said: "I ask neither sympathy nor compassion for the slaveholding states. We can take care of ourselves. It is not we, but the Union, which is in danger." This was said in the last year of Jackson's term, and Calhoun never swerved from these views. He was the prophet of the South and his opinions expressed in the Senate were as a gospel to its people. Again in 1850, four weeks before he died, he said: "I will say—and I say it boldly—that as things now stand the Southern states cannot remain in the Union." For him the Union had to be one that sheltered slavery; the South would remain in the Union only on its own terms.

Jackson lived to see the overthrow of his successor, Van Buren, the election of Harrison, the administrations of Tyler and Polk, and the annexation of Texas, in 1845, which he himself had so vigorously urged; and in that same year the "Hero of New Orleans" passed away in the seventy-eighth year of his age. Then followed the Presidencies of Taylor, Pierce, and Buchanan, each serving but one term, the last named being succeeded by Abraham Lincoln, whose election meant that the day of compromise in regard to the slavery issue was at an end. That this was felt to be so in the South and that the election of a Republican President would be the signal for the secession of the Southern states are evident from speeches made before and after that event in both Houses of Congress.

The speech of Martin J. Crawford of Georgia, delivered December 15, 1859, well expresses the feeling that was then dominant in the South. "To talk," said Crawford, "of the settlement of this slavery question is folly; to talk of a compromise upon this subject of slavery is worse than folly; . . . this question has resolved itself at last into a question of slavery and disunion, or no slavery and union. . . . I have this to say, and I speak the sentiment of every Democrat on this floor from the state of Georgia, we will never sub-

From *Harper's Magazine*, January, 1881

OLD-TIME SCHOOL IN PENNSYLVANIA

mit to the inauguration of a black Republican President." While the sentiment of the North was fittingly expressed in the speech of Hickman of Pennsylvania, an anti-Lecompton Democrat, who said: "The North will never tolerate a division of the territory. . . . I am neither a prophet nor the son of a prophet, but I express my belief that there is as much true courage in the North, though it may not be known by the name of chivalry, as there is in the South. . . . I believe . . . that, with all the appliances of art to assist, eighteen millions of men reared to industry, with habits of the right kind, will always be able to cope successfully, if need be, with eight millions of men without these auxiliaries."

Thus the issue was joined. The new Republican party, founded to prohibit slavery from occupying another inch of free territory, had elected its President. The North believed slavery to be wrong, and with the election of Lincoln the South abandoned all hope of slavery being taken under the fostering care of the Federal government. No further surrender would be made to the slave oligarchy. And feeling that their equality in the Union was destroyed, the Southern leaders determined to form a slave republic in the South. In voting for secession, however, the majority in the South acted upon the idea which T. R. R. Cobb gave voice to in the Georgia legislature, November 12, 1860, when he said that the South could "make better terms out of the Union than in it."

It is evident, therefore, that at this time the people of the South had no idea of a permanent withdrawal from the Union. Indeed, ninety-nine out of every hundred of the people still sincerely hoped some plan would be devised to heal the dissensions. But the feeling of ill will toward the North was widespread, and upon this the political leaders skillfully played, until "it developed," as Chadwick says in his *Causes of the Civil War*, "into a catching, sympathetic, emotional movement, before which reason vanished." Weeks before the election, South Carolina had taken steps pointing to secession, and on December 20, 1860, following Lincoln's election, made all hope of compromise impossible by passing the Ordinance of Secession. After this momentous action the succession of events was rapid. Before another month had passed four other states followed her example. Then, on April 12th of the next year, Fort Sumter in Charleston Harbor was fired upon and forced to surrender to the state of South Carolina. Up to this time many

1855.

[316]

in the North believed that a policy of moderation and of peace would yet lead to the restoration of the Union. But by striking the first blow the Confederacy made a fateful mistake, for, as President Lincoln, almost alone among his Cabinet, had foreseen, the effect of firing upon the flag was like that of an electric charge. Immediately an impulse for the Union vibrated throughout the North, arousing in all the determination to avenge the insult that the Southerners under another flag had offered to that of the United States. "Fort Sumter," as Emerson said, "crystallized the North into a unit and the hope of mankind was saved." "It was for this," says Chadwick, "the Union fought; the freeing of the blacks was but a natural and necessary incident. The assault upon Sumter was the knife driven by the hand of the South itself into the vitals of slavery."

Chapter VI

SILENT HEROES OF WAR

W HEN the news of the firing upon Fort Sumter had been received in the North," says Howard Pyle in *The Romance of An Ambrotype*, "the springtime, as though in response to the insult offered to the flag, seemed to have burst into a glorious bloom of flags that flamed everywhere their bright colors against the sky." On that memorable Monday, three days later, when President Lincoln issued his call to arms, and as a result the four slave states, Virginia in the van, realizing that force was now to be used by the Federal government, declared for secession; when the thousands of conservatives, among whom up to this time there was a strong Union sentiment, also rose as one man and joined the secession procession—the dove of peace took flight and there broke out a war, as Hosmer says in *The Appeal to Arms*, "determined and sanguinary almost beyond example."

Everywhere in all the cities, villages, and hamlets in the North and the South the streets were filled with people enthusiastic in support of their respective flags, for on both sides there was honest conviction as to the justice of their cause. In New Orleans, young and old, professional men and laborers, lawyers, doctors, and even the ministers, were all drilling. The shops there were closed at six so that the clerks could go to their drilling. The ladies held fairs, made clothes for the army, and animated the men by appeals to their chivalry and their patriotism to resist the enemy to the death. This same enthusiasm displayed at New Orleans, as Mrs. R. L. Hunt of New Orleans wrote to Secretary Chase,

The Midnight Court Martial

Illustration from
"WILLIAMS, C. S. A."
by William Gilmore Beymer

Originally published in
HARPER'S MAGAZINE, *September*, 1909

pervaded the whole South. In the North this same spirit had its counterpart. There also public meetings were held in every city, village, and hamlet, and in addressing the multitudes there assembled the speakers had no need to argue the right or wrong of the quarrel. The few glowing phrases of the watchwords and war cries in which were expressed the spirit of the people, such as "The Union must and shall be preserved," "Liberty and Union, now and forever, one and inseparable," and espe-

From *Harper's Magazine*, December, 1896

IN EVERY CITY, VILLAGE, AND HAMLET, MEN RUSHED TO THE RECRUITING STATION

cially the flag dispatch of Gen. John A. Dix, "If any man attempts to haul down the American flag, shoot him on the spot," personally addressed, as it seemed, to each citizen, answered all arguments. Those who had been lukewarm now rallied to resist; and in response to Lincoln's call recruits of the finest quality gathered fast.

Among the first to enlist were students from the schools and colleges, mere boys, who, under their teachers as officers, made up entire companies. But as in the South, laborers, mechanics, and clerks, with the business men who employed them, were equally inspired with the patriotic spirit and made haste to go to the recruiting offices. Many a father, too old to serve in the ranks, bravely marched with his boy to the recruiting office and saw him enrolled in the common cause. Among the rich and poor the same spirit prevailed. And as fathers parted with their sons, so did wives part with their husbands, both enthusiastic to sacrifice their feelings on the altar of their country's service. The thought of death did not enter into the minds of those who gave or of those who served.

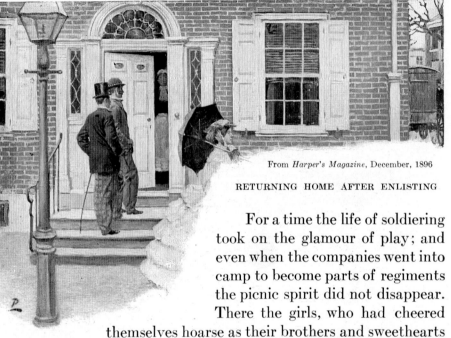

From *Harper's Magazine*, December, 1896

RETURNING HOME AFTER ENLISTING

For a time the life of soldiering took on the glamour of play; and even when the companies went into camp to become parts of regiments the picnic spirit did not disappear. There the girls, who had cheered themselves hoarse as their brothers and sweethearts marched off to camp, now came to visit them of an afternoon, making gay the canvas streets with the spread of their crinolines. Going from tent to tent, they liked to chat with the young officers now glorious in their new uniforms. Everything was quite gay, charming, and pleasant.

But this pleasantness was not to last long, and as the boys marched away from the towns to entrain for Washington, in spite of the cheering crowds of men and women that lined the sidewalks,

Jackson's Brigade Standing Like a Stone Wall
Before the Federal Onslaught at Bull Run

Illustration from
NON-COMBATANTS
by Robert W. Chambers

Originally published in
HARPER'S MAGAZINE, *November,* 1904

these troops on their way to the front were thinking of the grim business they were soon to face.

These first enthusiasts who rushed to enlist at Lincoln's call were for the most part without military training. But so great a clamor to strike a blow for the Union arose that, raw as they were, troops and leaders took the field at once, and that first summer of the war saw the two armies come to a death grapple on the battle-field of Bull Run.

THE CHARGE AT BULL RUN

At first the fortunes of the battle favored the Federals and the Confederates were driven in full retreat across the Warrington turnpike; but as they made their way up the slope of the Henryhouse hill, the brigade of Thomas A. Jackson stood "like a stone wall," calmly awaiting the Federal onslaught. There on the edge of the slope "Stonewall" Jackson, as he was ever afterward called, maintained his position, the leveled rifles of his brigade never silent, until the fresh troops of Joseph E. Johnston came upon the field and drove the Federals into full retreat, which soon became a rout, across the Virginia plains.

But the defeat at Bull Run only served to arouse the North to new energy, for, now realizing the war would be long and severe, volunteers flocked from far and wide and most of the men whose three months' period had expired re-enlisted. Those men who had not seen service at Bull Run were in the spring of the following year to receive their baptism of fire in the Peninsula campaign undertaken by McClellan in his attempt to capture Richmond. Upon the arrival of many of these new regiments at the Peninsula, the battle of Williamsburg, in which the Federals lost 456 killed and 1410 wounded, while the Confederate killed and wounded was 1570, had already begun. As the newly arrived regi-

From
Harper's Magazine, December, 1896
A FATHER GOING WITH HIS
BOY TO SEE HIM ENROLLED
IN THE COMMON CAUSE

[321]

ments advanced up the Yorktown road, they met wounded and sick men returning from the front, and lying close to the road along which they marched they saw the bodies of many dead men, dressed, like themselves, in dusty blue uniforms. These were dreadful sights for raw recruits to look upon, and all the while the noise of the battle grew louder and louder.

THE HORRORS OF WAR

But later on they would become used to the universal waste and destruction of war. Burning and ruined houses; the swollen, loathsome carcasses of horses; discarded wagons and cannon

From *Harper's Magazine*, December, 1896

THE GIRLS LIKED TO CHAT WITH THE YOUNG OFFICERS

abandoned as useless; the muskets, caps, and canteens of what had once been the glorious equipment of an army strewn everywhere along the roads; finally, more dead men who, like themselves, only a little while ago had been full of life—would become matters of course. Once they were marching along a beautiful Virginia countryside which destruction had not yet visited, and where all seemed calm and peaceful, when suddenly they saw the dead and wounded being brought on hay wagons into a house that stood off the road. As the stretchers were gotten ready they caught a glimpse of a sad-faced Southern girl with her little brother who stood watch-

They Brought in Their Dead and Wounded on
Hay Wagons

Illustration from
NON-COMBATANTS
by Robert W. Chambers

Originally published in
HARPER'S MAGAZINE, *November, 1904*

ing the pitiful sight, the girl so like the sister or sweetheart which each of them had left at home. Though she was a Southerner, like all women, her heart was tender and beneficent, and she cared kindly for the Union soldiers who were too sorely wounded to be moved. These marching men, however, were soldiers, and as such they must go on—on to their death, if necessary; and if wounded, depend upon being lifted into an ambulance and finally carried groaning to some hospital, there to lay selfish in their great sickness, their only feeling being one of relief that at last the roar of the battle had ceased.

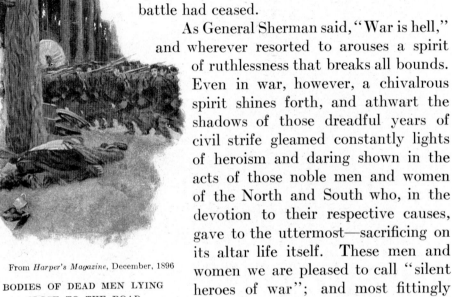

As General Sherman said, "War is hell," and wherever resorted to arouses a spirit of ruthlessness that breaks all bounds. Even in war, however, a chivalrous spirit shines forth, and athwart the shadows of those dreadful years of civil strife gleamed constantly lights of heroism and daring shown in the acts of those noble men and women of the North and South who, in the devotion to their respective causes, gave to the uttermost—sacrificing on its altar life itself. These men and women we are pleased to call "silent heroes of war"; and most fittingly so, for silently and unknown did

From *Harper's Magazine*, December, 1896

BODIES OF DEAD MEN LYING
CLOSE TO THE ROAD

they, as General Sheridan wrote in his reports, take "their lives in their hands, cheerfully going wherever ordered, to obtain that great essential of success, information." Of thirty or forty men once sent to obtain information upon which probably depended the fate of an army, Sherman had to report that "ten of these men were lost." "Of the ten," writes William Gilmore Beymer in his admirable work, *On Hazardous Service*, "no one of them died as do men in battle; two were found by their comrades hanging by their

The Secret Room

Illustration from
MISS VAN LEW
by William Gilmore Beymer

Originally published in
HARPER'S MAGAZINE, *June*, 1911

own halter straps; several more died like trapped animals, fighting desperately, at bay. And the others—never returned. Until the Great Book opens it will never be known where or how they died; they never returned, that is all. Of the ten, not a man was wearing the uniform of the country for which he died."

A MIDNIGHT COURT MARTIAL

These men were spies! At any rate, that was their legal status, for, disguised in the Confederate uniform, they penetrated the enemy's lines for the purpose of obtaining information. If taken, the swiftest and most terrible of all courts of law—a drumhead court martial, often held at midnight —would quickly decide their fate. No matter if they had no papers concealed upon their

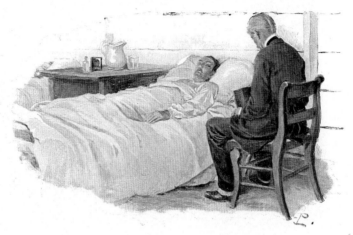

From *Harper's Magazine*, December, 1896
LYING WOUNDED IN THE HOSPITAL

persons, no matter if they had gained no information, the fact that they were caught in disguise within the enemy's lines made them subject, under strict military law, to the penalty of spies— ignominious death upon the gallows.

These men, however, are not to be considered in the light of professional spies who usually remained inside the enemy's lines and did not fight except in self-defense, often dishonorably betraying those whose hospitality they enjoyed. Such men were mere paid informers, who ply their trade in times of peace as well as of war and are justly held up to the everlasting obloquy of mankind. Of quite another stamp were these "silent heroes of war" whose adventures give to war the thrill and glamour of romance; who, in the face of great personal danger and at the risk of their lives, were within the enemy's lines day and night to obtain that great essential of success, "information."

It was this same "essential of success" which Washington so much desired when he begged his lieutenants to discover at all costs at what point the British intended to attack New York. "Leave no stone unturned," he wrote to General Heath, "nor do not stick at expense, to bring this to pass, as I was never more uneasy than on account of my want of knowledge on this score." But among the brave band of young officers to whom Colonel Knowlton made known the request of Washington, Nathan Hale was the only man to volunteer to undertake what all the others considered to be the work of a common spy. When his brother officers attempted to dissuade him from his purpose on the ground that he was exposing himself to an ignominious death, Hale replied:

"Gentlemen, I think I owe to my country the accomplishment of an object so important and so much desired by the commander of her armies, and I know no mode of obtaining the information but by assuming a disguise and passing into the enemy's camp. I am fully sensible of the consequences of discovery and capture in such a situation. But for a year I have been attached to the army and have not rendered any material service while receiving a compensation for which I make no return. Yet I am not influenced by any expectation of promotion or pecuniary reward. I wish to be useful; and every kind of service necessary for the public good becomes honorable by being necessary. If the exigencies of my country demand a peculiar service, its claims to the performance of that service become imperious."

As related earlier in this volume, Hale's disguise was uncovered; but he met his doom like a hero, convinced alike of the righteousness of his purpose and the justice of his country's cause, his last words on the gallows being, "I only regret that I have but one life to lose for my country."

Silent Heroes of War

Like Hale, the scouts of our Civil War who undertook hazardous service believed that "every kind of service necessary for the public good became honorable by being necessary." Moreover, the bravery of the Civil War scout (who insisted upon being called by that name, for gray clothes and all, he was not a *spy*) was more than physical—he was willing to do more than die for his cause. He was "willing," as Beymer says in *On Hazardous Service*, "to live through the pages of what men call History as a spy rather than make known his mission when caught and thus block the pathway of the man, and the man, and the man after that one, if need be, who he knew would follow him."

The daring men who made up the body known as army scouts were first obtained by special selection from different cavalry regiments. They were then assigned to what was called detached service. While on such

From *Harper's Magazine*, December, 1896
A SOLDIER CONVALESCING AT HOME

service it became their duty to reconnoiter or scout through the countryside between the lines, to carry orders—even though the battle was at its height—from one part of the field to another, "not looking for the safest route, but taking the most direct path, no matter how the bullets whistled." When their company was drawn up in line and the commander called for volunteers for "extra-dangerous duty," it was natural that from the ranks of such men, not one, but all, would step forward, each man fearful lest he might not be the one chosen for the perilous commission. As one of them said, "They wanted to know what was the 'extra-dangerous duty'"; and, when the men selected found out, they "hadn't the face to back down."

Such men as these, says Beymer, "seem to have been the nucleus of Sheridan's scouts in the Valley of the Shenandoah—

the Secret Service organization which a little later, having been recruited up to forty, under command of Major H. H. Young, became the most efficient, the most noted, in the Federal army." The heroic deeds of these men of the Secret Service—these "silent heroes of war," whose daring, unselfish work in the service of their country is scarcely mentioned in histories of the Civil War, are, however, brought to our attention in the imperishable record

From *Harper's Magazine*, December, 1896

A BEVY OF YOUNG GIRLS COME TO VISIT ONE OF THEIR BOYS INVALIDED HOME
FROM THE FRONT

written by General Sheridan in the brief words of his report of the expedition from Winchester to Petersburg, Virginia:

"To Maj. H. H. Young, of my staff, chief of scouts, and the thirty or forty men of his command, who took their lives in their hands, cheerfully going wherever ordered, to obtain that great essential of success, information, I tender my gratitude. Ten of these men were lost."

It is the glory of Beymer that in his admirable book he has told the stories of these men, among them Rowand, Young, and

She Was Continually Beset by Spies

Illustration from
MISS VAN LEW
by William Gilmore Beymer

Originally published in
HARPER'S MAGAZINE, *June,* 1911

Landegon, who, if ever men did, deserve the name of "faithful." Their stories have been told, in so far as such stories can ever be told, in order that what they did may be known, not as the deeds of spies, but as the acts of silent heroism which should be treasured by all who love to honor American heroes. But in the Secret Service there were women as well as men—women who did not move among the camps or ride across the battlefields, but who, nevertheless, obtained "that great essential of success, information," at even, if that be possible, greater risk and sacrifice than did the men. Among the women who rendered invaluable service to their cause on both sides in the Civil War, one of the most daring and deservedly the bravest was Elizabeth Van Lew, the story of whose faithfulness to the Union cause is so sympathetically told by Mr. Beymer.

MISS VAN LEW

On a bronze tablet set in the face of a great gray stone in the Shockhoe Hill Cemetery of Richmond, Virginia, there is carved the inscription:

Elizabeth L. Van Lew

1818   1900

She risked everything that is dear to man— friends, fortune, comfort, health, life itself, all for the one absorbing desire of her heart—that slavery might be abolished and the Union preserved

———

This Boulder from the Capitol Hill in Boston is a tribute from Massachusetts friends

"Miss Van Lew, a Richmond woman, was a spy for the Federal government," having, as General Grant said, sent him "the most valuable information received from Richmond during the war. "For four long years, without respite, she faced death to obtain that information; day after day suspected, spied upon, threatened, persecuted, she worked with a courage far higher than the excitement-mad valor of battlefields.

"The greater part of the military information received from Richmond by the Army of the Potomac was collected and transmitted by Miss Van Lew" through a chain of secret stations which she established for forwarding her cipher dispatches, the Richmond end of the chain being the old Van Lew mansion.

THE SECRET ROOM

"There she received and harbored the secret agents who stole in from the Federal army; when no Federal agents could reach her she sent her own servants as messengers through the Confederate armies. There," in the secret room "in the Van Lew house in the heart of Richmond, she concealed [and gave food to] many of the escaped Union prisoners from Castle Thunder, Libby, and Belle Isle; there she planned aid for those who remained in the prisons, to whom she sent or carried food and books and clothing; for their relief she poured out her money—thousands of dollars—until all her convertible property was gone. . . .

"In her childhood she was sent North to school—to Philadelphia, her mother's early home. There, a schoolgirl, she accepted those principles which were to determine the course of her whole life; she went back at last to Virginia an unwavering abolitionist. She gave freedom to nine of the Van Lew slaves; others were bought, that they might be reunited with a husband or a wife already in the Van Lew possession."

A few days after Lincoln issued his call to arms, Virginia passed the Ordinance of Secession, and troops began to pour in from other states until Virginia became one great military camp. "The ladies of Richmond sewed and knitted for the Confederacy and shot with pistols at a mark; Miss Van Lew wrote dispatches for the Union—specific information of Confederate troops, their numbers and their movements . . . the dispatches [going] north by special messenger. So the hot tumultuous days of summer passed; Bull Run was fought and Richmond for the first time filled with wounded South-

A Lonely Duel in the Middle of a Great
Sunny Field

Illustration from
ROWAND
by William Gilmore Beymer

Originally published in
HARPER'S MAGAZINE, *June*, 1909

ern men and wretched Northern prisoners. Here at last was work to do; from one official to another she hurried, begging that she might nurse the wounded Union soldiers, until at last, from General Winder, Provost-Marshal-General of Richmond, she obtained 'permission to visit the prisoners and to send them books, luxuries, delicacies, and what she may wish.' Thus her four years' service began.

"The Libby prison was her special care; it stood at the base of Church Hill, almost beneath her very door. There, in command, she found Lieutenant Todd, brother of Mrs. Lincoln, and won his 'kind feelings' for herself by gifts of buttermilk and gingerbread. Castle Thunder—'Particular Hell'—with Caphart—'Antichrist Caphart'—in control; Belle Isle in its stockade lying like a bleached bone in the midst of the turbulent river—for four bitter years she was known at them all.

"From the moment that she gained access to the prisoners her dispatches to the government increased a hundredfold in accuracy and value; for, though her hospital and prison ministrations were sincere

From *Harper's Magazine*, December, 1896

A SOLDIER VISITING HIS SWEETHEART
BEFORE RETURNING TO THE FRONT

and genuine for humanity's sake, they were also a cloak to cover her real mission; Miss Van Lew above all else was a spy."

In the prisons "she had little trouble with the soldiery; 'Crazy Bett,' they called her, and let her wander about almost at will; they laughed as she passed singing softly to herself or muttering meaningless words." And so "Crazy Bett" she became to the soldiers and minor officials; but to the "people of Richmond she was still Miss Van Lew, a Southern woman who had turned against her neighbors and against the South; and as the war lengthened and bore more heavily upon them, their resentment turned to implacable hatred."

CONSTANTLY BESET BY SPIES

The likelihood of her detection now seemed inevitable. Extreme caution became necessary, for Confederate spies were everywhere. As she writes in her diary: "If you spoke in your parlor or chamber to your next of heart, you whispered, you looked under the lounges and beds. . . . Visitors apparently friendly were treacherous. They [we] were publicly denounced, and walked the streets for four years as shunned lepers. . . . I shall ever remember the pale face of this dear lady [her mother]—her feeble health; her dread of Castle Thunder and Salisbury—for her arrest was constantly spoken of, and frequently reported on the street, and some never hesitated to say she should be hanged. . . . Unionists lived ever in a reign of terror—I was afraid even to pass the prison; I have had occasion to stop near it when I dared not look up at the windows. I have turned to speak to a friend and found a detective at my elbow. Strange faces could sometimes be seen peeping around the columns and pillars of the back portico."

Thus for four long years she lived a life of peril, in constant danger of being discovered and dying the death of a spy. But Miss Van Lew never ceased to scheme and plan until victory came to her cause.

Only for a time, however, did the government she so faithfully served remember her. President Grant appointed her postmistress of Richmond and for "eight years she conducted the office with competence, even skill; her business relations with the people of Richmond were for the most part amicable, but socially she paid, she paid!

"'I live—and have lived for years—as entirely distinct from the citizens as if I were plague-stricken,' she wrote. 'Rarely, very rarely, is our door-bell ever rung by any but a pauper or those desiring my service. . . . September, 1875, my mother was taken from me by death. We had not friends enough to be pall-bearers.'"

Her persecutors, however, hounded her so that when Hayes became President she lost her place. There followed years of

The Siege of Vicksburg

During the siege of Vicksburg the non-combatants who took refuge in the caves dug in the hillside for their protection had many narrow escapes from the shells thrown into the city by the besieging fleet.

Illustration from
A CHILD AT THE SIEGE OF VICKSBURG
by William W. Lord, Jr.

Originally published in
HARPER'S MAGAZINE, *December*, 1908

distressing poverty until finally she obtained a clerkship in the Post Office Department at Washington. But when the war party was overthrown she was made to feel that she owed her place to "sentimental reasons," that her "peculiar temperament" rendered her "a hindrance to the other clerks," and finally, when she was called "a troublesome relict" she wrote her resignation. Thus "a heartbroken old woman, she returned to the lonely house on Church Hill," where, a few years later, "nursed by an old negress to whom she had given freedom long years before," she died. As Mr. Beymer says, "There is but one paragraph more to be written—to be copied from a torn scrap of paper among her manuscripts:

"'If I am entitled to the name of "Spy" because I was in the Secret Service, I accept it willingly; but it will hereafter have to my mind a high and honorable signification. For my loyalty to my country I have two beautiful names—here I am called "Traitor," farther North a "Spy"—instead of the honored name of "Faithful."'"

ROWAND

Of the brave band of thirty or forty men who formed Sheridan's Secret Service organization in the Valley of the Shenandoah, thanks to Mr. Beymer, we know something of the heroic work of three of the most daring—Rowand, Landegon, and Young. It was to the last named, Major Harry Young, his chief of scouts, that Sheridan wrote in March, 1865, tendering his gratitude for their "invaluable" work, adding, "Ten of these men were lost."

"How many men went down in the remaining twelve days of the war," Beymer writes, he does not know—"those twelve savage days that saw Five Forks and Sailor's Creek, Dinwiddie Court House, Deep Creek, Farmville, and Appomattox Station and the Court House; those days when the scouts worked night and day and were in their own lines only long enough to give 'information.'"

It was in the fall of 1862 that Rowand, then a member of a West Virginia cavalry company, had volunteered "for extra-dangerous duty, just to see what was extra dangerous about it, and

Sheridan's First Interview with Rowand

Illustration from
ROWAND
by William Gilmore Beymer

Originally published in
HARPER'S MAGAZINE, *June*, 1909

had stepped forward—into the gray uniform." From then on he did much rough scouting, through rugged West Virginia, becoming dispatch bearer for General Milroy, whose messages he carried to Halltown, West Virginia, wildly riding amid the bursting shells.

But it was in the Valley of the Shenandoah, where Archibald H. Rowand was known as "Barefoot" Rowand of "the Valley," that he felt most at home, "and he was glad when he was ordered back to report there to General Averell in the fall." While serving as Averell's chief scout he had many exciting adventures, and never failed in obtaining that great essential of success, information, though many times he came near to being hanged in doing so.

A LONELY DUEL IN THE MIDDLE OF A GREAT, SUNNY FIELD

"He told of a lonely duel in the middle of a great, sunny field. There was neither sight nor sound of armies or of war: only summer sights and sounds—wind in the long grass, and bees; and the great white clouds overhead. And he was going toward the rebel lines, and that other boy was headed for the lines of the blue. Each knew that the other must not go; they fired. Of all the memories of those harsh, savage days, the one of most bitter regret is that of the lonely, sunlit field where lay the huddled body of the other boy."

SHERIDAN'S FIRST INTERVIEW WITH ROWAND

This was the last scouting Rowand did for Averell. "Then Sheridan came to the Valley. His coming meant much to the nation; it meant much to Rowand, too. It meant the opportunity to do work that was of great value to his flag; it meant such an increase of the dangers and excitement he loved as to make most of what had gone before seem but playing. For him it meant friendship—almost intimacy—with this greatest of cavalry generals; and a hero worship begun as a boy has continued to this day.

"From their first interview Sheridan seemed to take to the boy, perhaps for his very boyishness, perhaps for his audacity and independence of speech, as much as for his cool daring in his work.

[335]

'I'd like to report to you personally, General, or not at all; if not, please send me to my regiment,' he said at that interview. This was because under Averell the scouts reported to Major Howe, who repeated the reports to the general. He got one of Rowand's mixed; as a consequence Averell lost a number of men, and angrily ordered Rowand to his regiment in disgrace. Rowand was able to prove he had reported correctly and that he had reached a certain point (he proved it by the dead body of his comrade, who fell at that place). After that he refused to report except to Averell, and his demand was acceded to. He meant to start right with Sheridan.

"'I wanted to stay with Averell; begged to stay. He said he was sorry to lose me, but that I would have to go. I went, accordingly. I had never seen General Sheridan, never had him described. Averell and Milroy were big men—somehow I expected to find another big man; he was big only in fight. (Sheridan was but five feet five.) He was pointed out to me in front of headquarters, and I went up and saluted. He looked me up and down.

"'"I asked General Averell for his oldest scout," was all he said.

"'"I am his oldest in point of service—in knowledge of the Valley," I answered.

"'"How old are you? How long have you served?" he inquired. I was nineteen, I told him, and had scouted for over two years in the Valley. He took me into headquarters and pumped me for an hour and a half; then sent me for four or five good men as "quick as you can get them. . . ."

"'Months afterward General Sheridan asked me what I supposed he saw when I first reported to him: "Two big brown eyes and a mouth, Rowand; that was all!" I weighed less than a hundred and forty then—you mightn't believe it now—and I was six feet tall. He had that way with us, that easy friendliness; we would have done anything for him. He was a fine man!'"

Of the closing days of the war, when he was around Petersburg, Rowand might have told many stories, but as he said, "Every proper story should have a climax, and this is the climax of mine. I missed the Grand Review! I had to leave Washington the very day before."

LANDEGON

Equally as daring as Rowand was John Landegon, that other "silent hero," and fully as brave, for it was of him that General Kilpatrick used to say: "He was the bravest man I ever knew." In his native village they would not enlist him. "He was too young, too thin, too poor food for powder." But in the neighboring town of Waterbury, Connecticut, where they were growing anxious to fill the town's quota, they took him, under age and all as he was. It was thus that John Landegon went to war. Craving excitement and finding camp life monotonous, he often stole out beyond the picket lines and wandered among the fields and woods of "no man's land," where he more than once saw "long, black lines creeping along the side of a distant hill." One day that he had wandered out farther than ever before, from "among the trees he caught a glimpse of moving gray" that came straight on to the tree behind which he stood. "Behind lay the Confederate army—he could not run." The man was a young Confederate officer "returning from some lone-hand scout of his own," and when he "was almost to the tree" Landegon, levelling his musket, sprang out at him, and marched him a captive back to camp. After that he went on all the scoutings that were made.

The getting of information and the carrying of messages were done at the risk of his life, yet, such hazardous tasks were merely part of the day's work for this "silent hero of war." He knew that the success of his cause depended upon his getting through, and to accomplish that no risk was too great. But one day he came near being hanged, and at Mr. Beymer's prompting he related this adventure.

"'Do you know that there are nights even yet when I dream of that day? Do you know—but, of course, you don't! Well, you've got me to thinking of it again, and I might as well tell you, even of that, too.

"'There was a cavalry skirmish a couple of miles from Massaponax Church—about twelve or fifteen miles south of Fredericksburg; it was going hard against us, and I was sent back to bring up help. I was about halfway to the church when I saw a lot of dust, and I rode harder—thinking, you understand, it was the advance of some of our troops; there was so much dust that I rode right into them before I found that they were Confederates that had got round our flank and were coming up behind our men. It was just a scouting party . . . more coming, I learned. There wasn't a chance to get away, or even to fight; they had never made any mistake about me . . . grabbed me the minute I got in reach. I was in my gray uniform, mind! They were in a hurry, but they said they had time to hang me. They just hauled off to the roadside and said they would have a trial, anyway—that they always tried the men they hanged. So they got up a drumhead court that wasn't any more a court than is our talking here. . . .

"'The president of the court got up and said, "You're guilty, Yank, and it is the sentence of this court that we hang you by the neck until you're dead. . . ."

"'So they dragged and lifted me on to a horse, and led it under the limb, and they put the noose around my neck. I didn't see anything or think anything from the time I got put on the horse, and I didn't see that some of them were standing in a little party off to one side. Just then one stepped out and said that I was not to be hung, that I was a brave man; and it wasn't so much that they didn't want me to be hanged, but the other fellows weren't going to do it; I was as much their prisoner as I was theirs—that they hadn't any of them been selected for the court; . . . more of that sort of thing (they were from two regiments—do you understand?) and that they had decided to send me back to the main column and have me tried right! Some of the fellows drew their revolvers, and some got on their horses, and it looked as if there was going to be a fight right there. But they talked it over—with me sitting on the horse and the rope around my neck all the time—and finally decided that they would send me on.

[338]

"They Talked It Over—With Me Sitting
on the Horse"

Illustration from
LANDEGON
by William Gilmore Beymer

Originally published in
HARPER'S MAGAZINE, *November,* 1909

"'They took the rope off and I began to get some of my senses back, and I saw that the man who was to take me forward was a great, surly-looking devil—one of them that had been so anxious to hang me; he was standing talking to his officer, and they looked over at me, and he kind of smiled and nodded his head; I knew right there that he meant to kill me on the way—was getting ordered to just then.

"'We started—he and I—and the others rode away. . . .

"'I kept on the off side of the horse, so that he would have to cut across with his saber instead of down, when the time came for me to try to run. I can see that road now—long and straight, with the unfenced fields sloping down to the road on either side, and sumac bushes along where the fences had been before the war; ahead, the road ran like a tunnel into a big woods that looked all hazy and blue. Beyond the woods a little way was Massaponax Church; I made up my mind that what was to be would take place in that woods, and I sort of felt that the Confederate had made up his mind to end it in the woods, too.

"'Just then he called to me: "Halt, Yank! till I tighten the girth—saddle's slippin'!"

"'He was dismounting—you know, of course, how a man gets off a horse? his left foot in the stirrup, and swings his right leg back over the horse; for just a second his back was toward me, and at that moment he dropped his drawn saber to the ground. . . . He died right there!'"

YOUNG

Now a few words about Major Harry Young, Sheridan's chief of scouts, under whom both Rowand and Landegon served in the Valley of the Shenandoah—he who, like these other "silent heroes of war," found camp life irksome and went out between the lines to quicken it. He of whom Sheridan said, "I *want* him!" and General Edwards, from whose command Sheridan got him, "I would rather you would take my right arm than to have you take him from me." Finally the tribute of his own men, who said, "We think God A'mighty of him."

The American Spirit

"THE NATION IS AT WAR AND MUST HAVE MEN"

As Mr. Beymer writes: "It is like a picture—that first story that begins before he was a soldier; the dusty chaise in which there stands the boy Young . . . and at his side the solemn-eyed little girl of ten, breathlessly watching brother Henry as he talks . . . forgetful of the very crowd that hems them in and that stands with upturned, troubled faces. He is saying, 'The nation is at war and must have men.'" And "so, through the Blackstone Valley, in every village, the boy calls a crowd about him, and at the end of one day's haranguing sixty-three men have volunteered to enlist with him." He himself, however, was not taken, for when he brought the list to the recruiting office Rhode Island's quota had already been filled. But on June 6, 1861, Colonel Slocum sent for him, and "he was mustered in with the regiment as Company B's second lieutenant."

From the very beginning his daring and bravery attracted the attention of his superiors, so that he soon received a staff appointment; and with it, "he began his self-taught, self-sought apprenticeship to the Secret Service." In 1864 he became Col. Oliver Edwards's inspector-general, and while serving in that capacity he performed a deed of daring which caused General Sheridan to say, "I *want* him!"

The regular scouts having failed to obtain reliable information regarding a suspected attack of the enemy, the dauntless Major Young undertook to find out what they were up to. With three picked men and himself and four Confederate cavalry uniforms, he proposed to "join the enemy's marching column and ride with them until he had gained the information." Such a feat was considered impossible, but "Henry Harrison Young tried the impossible and succeeded." Six hours later, "when he dismounted at Edwards's headquarters, he bore full information of the plans of the enemy."

No wonder Sheridan wanted him! Young at once proceeded to organize his new command—Sheridan's Secret Service in the Valley of the Shenandoah. "The war was within five months of the end, but into that time there was crowded more work by the

"The Nation Is at War and Must Have Men"

Illustration from
YOUNG
by William Gilmore Beymer

Originally published in
HARPER'S MAGAZINE, *December,* 1909

Secret Service than had been done in all the years that preceded." When the war ended, five months later, "there were few enough to answer 'present.' That there were any at all is the wonder after such service as this"—the attack of Young and his less than sixty men upon an entire brigade of Confederate cavalry; the capture of Major Harry Gilmor, whose guerilla bands always were upon the skirts of the Union army, cutting off detachments, stragglers, and all trains not strongly guarded.

Mr. Beymer tells how "Young was given the opportunity to snatch from certain death unreckoned scores of Union soldiers, condemned that hour to lay their lives down for their flag.

"There would," he writes, "be given the name of the skirmish (which in any other war would be dignified by the name of battle), but the name is lost in the crowded memories of the few who knew the story. But perhaps there will be, of those who wore the blue, one who will read this story to whom there will come back the memory of a morning with the regiments that lay on their faces at the wood's edge, galled and torn by the shells constantly bursting among them, while they awaited, restive, the order for the charge across the open and the attempt to scale the hillside from whose all but impregnable crest the battery thundered. Others there are, of the South, who will recall with heartburnings the loss of an all-but-won engagement. Here, perhaps for the first time, they will learn the reason. Some may now recollect having seen in the driving smoke a boyish, gray-clad officer who, in the name of their commanding general, ordered the battery to take immediate position on the left flank—there to be utterly useless. Perhaps they recall the way he sat his horse, there amid the flying Federal bullets, until he saw the carrying out of his orders; then that they had seen him gallop away, forever, leaving them, the dupes, to face their angered general.

"Young had carried to the Federal regiment the order to take the battery—the key position of the engagement; he had seen the terrible slaughter which must be the price of success, and he had not given the order. Instead he had formed a plan and told it;

General Lee on His Famous Charger, "Traveler"

Illustration from
GENERAL LEE AS I KNEW HIM
by A. R. H. Ranson
Originally published in
HARPER'S MAGAZINE, *February,* 1911

They Awaited the Order to Charge

Illustration from
YOUNG
by William Gilmore Beymer

Originally published in
HARPER'S MAGAZINE, *December,* 1909

then swiftly donning his gray uniform and making a detour, he had entered the Confederate lines, at no one knows what hazard, and had come up behind the battery, to whose captain he had given a false order. The astonished Federal soldiers rushed the abandoned hill crest before the Confederates could replace their guns; but as for Major Young, an unexpected shift in the position of the army compelled him to remain within the Confederate lines for hours, in imminent danger of detection and capture—and death. . . . "

In the case of Harry Young, however, "capture and death never had far to come, for he was always at least halfway to meet them." The same can be as truly said of his companions in the Secret Service—those "silent heroes of war" who, like Nathan Hale, were willing to bear the name of spies, believing, like their great prototype, that "every kind of service necessary for the public good becomes honorable by being necessary."

HIS ARMY BROKE UP AND FOLLOWED HIM, WEEPING AND SOBBING

But at last, and in no small measure due to the devoted, self-sacrificing work of these silent heroes—of Rowand, Landegon, Young, and Elizabeth Van Lew, and many others like them—the terrible conflict came to an end when on Sunday, April 9, 1865, Gen. Robert E. Lee rode out of his own lines to meet General Grant in the McLean House, at Appomattox Court House. The cause of his going was well known to all of his men, although not a word had been spoken; and when he rode back into his own lines, as A. R. H. Ranson writes in *Harper's Magazine*, February, 1911, in his article, "General Lee As I Knew Him," "erect and grand—grander than ever—his army broke up into a loving mob and followed him, holding on to his hands, his feet, his coat, the bridle of his horse and its mane, weeping and sobbing as if their hearts would break." Thus did they show their great love for him, although he had come back to them after having just signed the letter in which he surrendered the Army of Northern Virginia—"from signing away the existence of the Confederate States of America."

Abraham Lincoln

Illustration from
LINCOLN'S LAST DAY
by William H. Crook

Originally published in
HARPER'S MAGAZINE, *September,* 1907

His Army Broke Up and Followed Him, Weeping
and Sobbing

Illustration from
GENERAL LEE AS I KNEW HIM
by A. R. H. Ranson

Originally published in
HARPER'S MAGAZINE, *February,* 1911

Thus ended the Civil War, and with the close of the bloody conflict an end came to brothers fighting brothers, the outcome of which was the triumph of the Union. As James Russell Lowell wrote after Appomattox: "The news is from heaven. I wanted to laugh and I wanted to cry, and ended by holding my peace and feeling devoutly thankful. There is something magnificent in having a country to love. It is almost like what one feels for a woman. Not so tender, perhaps, but to the full as self-forgetful." Well might this news have come from heaven, for, as J. K. Hosmer writes in his *Outcome of the Civil War*, "the war settled not only that the Union should persist, but that its cornerstone should be freedom. [And now] among the nations of the earth, there is not one whose foundations seem more stable, a stability which North and South are equally anxious to maintain."

The war had many victims, both in the North and in the South, among whom the most illustrious was Abraham Lincoln, the greatest of all the "silent heroes of war," without whose patience, resolution, judgment, and devotedness the Union could not have been preserved.

THE END